Dean Sampson

My Shangri-La

Dean Sampson

My Shangri-La

Dave Sampson and Dean Sampson

Vertical Editions

First published in the United Kingdom in 2003 by Vertical Editions,
18-20 Blackwood Hall Lane, Luddendenfoot, Halifax HX2 6HD

ISBN 1-904091-04-0

Jacket design and typeset by HBA, York

Printed and bound by CPI Bookcraft, Midsomer Norton

Contents

Acknowledgements

I would like to convey my thanks to a number of people who have helped me in the writing of this book and indeed throughout my life and career. Firstly my friends and family without who none of this would have been possible and especially my wife and my mum for the love and encouragement they have always given me and my dad who has helped me greatly in my playing career and for the huge effort he has made writing much of this book.

Special mention must also go to Peter Smith at the Yorkshire Evening Post for his support through the years and for agreeing to write the foreword for this book, to Sig Kasatkin for supplying many of the photos and making many rugby league players, myself included, look like heroes, to Len Garbutt for assistance with facts and figures and to Stuart Raper, John Kear, Mick Morgan, Richard Wright and Adrian Vowles for their tributes published on the last few pages. I didn't pay them for their comments – honest!

I would also like to acknowledge my teammates, coaches and all the backroom staff with every club and team I have played for; from Castleford to Australia and the national sides as well. Without them, my career would not have been the adventure it has turned out to be and they have certainly helped make my story worth telling.

And last but not least, a big thanks is due to all those loyal fans especially at Castleford, it is their loyal support that has made the whole adventure so worthwhile. I just hope a few can identify with my story and enjoy reading it as much as my dad and I have enjoyed writing it.

Dean Sampson

Foreword

As rugby league writer for the Yorkshire Evening Post, I've developed an annual pre-season ritual. Every February I trot down to Castleford Tigers media day and chat to Dean Sampson about definitely, absolutely, certainly his final season as a rugby league player. Fortunately, the old warhorse has kept on going and no one who saw him help turn an 18-0 deficit into an incredible 36-22 win against St Helens in May 2002 could claim Dean has played on past his best. But now Diesel has finally hung up his boots, and it's the end of an era for the Castleford club, where he has become an almost legendary figure. Dean is one of the last of the true one-club men. Under the new freedom of contract, the days of players, especially good ones like Dean, spending their entire career with just one club are almost certainly over and the sport will be the poorer for that. With more than 400 games under his belt, Dean has written himself a place in Castleford folklore, it is just a pity his efforts weren't given greater recognition by the international selectors. One substitute appearance for Great Britain and five England caps are meagre reward for someone who has been among the best and most consistent props in domestic competition in three different decades. In sixteen years at Castleford, Dean has tasted at least as many highs as lows, but his determination to stay loyal to the club which gave him his break says a lot about the man. It was unfortunate that Dean joined Tigers just after their last Wembley success, in 1986. When Castleford lost to Wigan in a Challenge Cup semi-final in 2002, it was noticeable that Dean's team mates were just as disappointed for him, having seen his final chance of a cup winner's medal disappear, as they were for themselves. There's no doubting Dean's contribution to the Castleford cause on the field, but he's also been a great ambassador off it, there's an old cliché that rugby league props are not to put too fine a point on it, thick. As a reporter always in search of a quote, I've learned that the exact opposite is true, they are often the most eloquent, deep thinking and approachable players in a team. Dean is no exception, if Castleford have lost and the mood in the dressing room is black, he can always be relied upon to put an honest, insightful perspective on what's just happened. He's also good for a laugh, as proved after once telling me: 'If Cas lose this weekend's game, I'll do my next Evening Post interview naked.' Of course, Cas preceded to lose miserably to Widnes Vikings and Diesel was as good as his word, posing in next day's paper with his modesty protected only by a copy of the Evening Post. Diesel is certainly no angel, as his disciplinary record proves and occasionally he's copped for the wrong sort of headlines, but typically he's taken that on the chin and never borne a grudge. Dean's success coaching in the amateur ranks at Stanley Rangers suggest he will still have a role to fill in rugby league now his playing days have finally come to an end, so his story may be far from over, up to now, it's been a terrific ride and I'm delighted he's decided to record it all for posterity.

Peter Smith
Yorkshire Evening Post

1

Let the Good Times Roll

Many who have read Dad's book 'Fast Lane to Shangri-La' will, I feel, put the inevitable question to me - have you ever-visited Dean? Well I can answer quite categorically, yes - on several occasions in different manners and for different reasons but whilst these trips and the memories of them are to be treasured. I won't forget the occasional trips I have also made to hell, at least that's where I felt I was at that particular time. And allow me to point out the vast gulf in the two journeys from a throne to the gutter, euphoria to despair. The pressures on the modern athlete are easing as more and more come through the system from an early age and have never known any different. But when Super League came along in the mid-nineties, many athletes were halfway through their careers and the call to adapt to full-time professionalism and the extra restrictive and rigorous lifestyle it brought about were a culture shock to many. Some of us were lucky, I feel under Darryl Van de Velde we had a head start, his demands and rigorous regimental approach had been our hors d' oeuvre before the main meal. Nevertheless, many players had varying problems, some fell by the wayside quickly, others a little later, some partially adapted, a few took it in their stride and positively relished the new found wealth and profile full time involvement brought with it. Super League made us superstars and I must say I feel it made me personally

11

a better player. But as a team, whilst we had some good seasons at Castleford, when push came to shove we probably under achieved, falling short of netting the big prizes on offer.

Looking back in time - something I am now able to do having reached the age of thirty-five and having played my final Super League season - it does not seem almost twenty years ago that I started with the juniors playing under the banner of Pointer Panthers under seventeen's. That's a fact though and despite many highs and lows, I have no regrets. However, I'm keen to stay at Castleford as long as possible and progress into coaching, so I was chuffed when the club offered me a dual role in my last season both playing for the first team and developing the juniors.

Now ours is a family steeped in top-level sport since 1957, when my uncle Malcolm signed for Wakefield Trinity and set the yardstick for the rest of us to follow. Since then, there has been a Sampson playing top-flight rugby to this day. When I retire, the responsibility will fall to my cousin Paul, he plays t'other game as my granddad used to call it, and plays at the highest level with London's premier club Wasps and has represented England at both full international and in the sevens at the Manchester Commonwealth Games. For a time he played at Wakefield Trinity and I hope some day he has another dabble at rugby league. With luck, he could play into the next epoch, and then the ever-burning flame may be handed on to my son - Joseph George Hallas Sampson. Only five years old, but a bloody huge lad, he really is going to be awesome!

Family life and traditions are something my dad has taught us always to be proud of no matter how high or low your origins. In fact, I believe from lowly origins you can, with determination, aspire to unimaginable heights. If one takes an example of say rugby league, it is now universally agreed by intellectuals (well the unbiased ones) to be up there with the Olympians of athleticism. Full-time and Super League advancements have brought us to a standard that would have been incomprehensible a century ago when the well documented acrimonious breakaway took place and working class people went professional - albeit part-time. The mere fact that they honed well-muscled finely tuned torsos by sheer hard graft – well, I suppose I'm lucky I've never had to experience such hardship. Anyway, working conditions have improved and, in my opinion, so has the game. Maybe others will disagree, and I'm not going to argue, I've done that enough with Dad about the subject and we beg to differ but certainly the profile of rugby league has never been higher.

The formation of BARLA and the concept of the Conference League have evolved our once parochial sport in three northern counties to a now more national one. But whilst not loosing sight of the massive challenge ahead of us, never has the platform for success been as solid.

Being the son of a publican and a member of a family steeped in rugby league, I've heard most of my life comments such as: 'tha naw's tint as good as it wah' or 'tha couldn't a lived wi so an so.' Well maybe so, maybe not. I admire and respect older fans and players opinions, but that's just it - it's all about opinions. But I think Dad's already covered this and many other stories from rugby league days long gone, so read his book for more on the subject.

I'll say no more about that particular subject, but what I do know from the research Dad did for his book is that going back in time from my granddad, I have at least ten generations of mining stock behind me. The thinking in the family is that the Sampson's probably originated from the tin mines of Cornwall, which is no doubt why my more recent ancestors went down the pit in Yorkshire. Going further back, Dad's investigations suggest the family came over to Cornwall from France. In fact he argues that our name is of biblical origin from Samson who miffed those Arabs so long ago by having an affair with Delilah and then slaying 2,000 Philistines with the jawbone of an ass. Dad reckons the authorities would have been more than a bit pissed off and so everyone carrying the name would have upped and done a runner, a long runner, maybe to France, and then on to Cornwall, where anyone bearing the name could only get manual labour in the tin mines. Our name does get a mention in the Doomsday book in 1086 and Hugo Samson is mentioned in the Pipe Rolls for Northamptonshire in 1130 and William Samson in the Assize Rolls for Cheshire in 1260 then nothing for 500 years - it must have taken us that long to re-emerge in Yorkshire. To this day the name is more common in Cornwall, Devon, Kent and Derbyshire, so I know where to spend my holidays! It also seems the family motto in Latin is Dexis Letho Flagibum, which I believe when translated (not by me) means 'red wrath rising'. Hey temper, temper Mum used to say, now I know why.

On my mum's side, much of the family originates from around the Lake District, so maybe if Cumbria were allowed back into the Cross County Challenge games, I would qualify with my maternal granddad being Cumbrian. Now I'd really like that - not that I'm not proud of being a Yorkshireman, but seeing as my ancestors seem to originate from all over the place, well I suppose you can understand my confusion. Anyway, Graham Steadman has just quoted 'we are picking the men in form for Yorkshire,' except me that is, even though as I write this

I'm in the OPTA form team of the month, I'm excluded - I'm too old. It seems that the adage 'if your good enough your old enough' which is often directed to youngsters breaking into the game, doesn't apply to the older players. It gives food for thought; I certainly don't feel too old and would dearly love a crack at those Aussies in a one-off test. Nevertheless, it's not to be and I find the hierarchy's attitude to age inconsistent with what we are trying to achieve.

When Wayne Bennett the Australian guru on coaching rewards Allan Langer and Andrew Gee former Aussie internationals with places in their State of Origin series, he wasn't questioned in the press and media over their ages and its contribution to the future of the Aussie game. Bennett must have believed that these two players would offer much to the other young members of the squad that he as a coach could not. I thought Andrew Gee more so than Allan Langer looked overweight and past his best with Warrington last season, but the obvious carrot offered by Bennett by the look of his new slimline appearance on TV must have inspired a last hurrah. And with the interchange system used wisely, his presence was visibly measurable and no doubt they both made off field contributions too. I certainly think that Bennett gave the team a better chance of winning by using Langer's experience and organisational skills and Gee for his presence and solid reliability. Maybe we should start using another adage in the game - 'there's life in the old dog yet'.

Anyway, in the recent one-off test, we placed the task of taking the Aussies on up front with two natural props in Terry O'conner and Barrie McDermott. I feel we needed four especially as Barrie is used by Leeds in twenty minute spells. It was too big an ask of them against the power and pace of Webke, Stevens, Ryles and Co and from the comfort of my armchair I felt for our boys. Keiron Cunningham could not be expected to maintain his early busy involvement after being out injured for so long, Andy Farrell also did not look 100% fit, neither did Paul Wellens and let's remember these are our world class players. They apparently carried injuries into such a big game played only a few days after arriving, well my sympathy went out to all our lads and I'm not looking to make excuses, just offering reasons. One thing that did stick out a mile was we were outplayed in every department, our kicking game was abysmal and our inability to gain good field position embarrassing. Our two props got over the gain line consistently but apart from an occasional Paul Sculthorpe burst (who I felt was outstanding), we seemed devoid of craft and organisation. Perhaps that's down to lack of enough preparation time, but only the players and coaching staff know the answer because I think we are not as far behind the Aussies as this game would have us believe.

So this brings us to the age-old question, what can we do to fully compete at an international level? Well the first and most obvious step, controversial as it may sound, is limit the number of Aussies over here. This won't make me the most popular guy in rugby but it's my belief that our youngsters are hitting a dead end when approaching Super League standards and inevitably drop to the NFP without ever getting a sustained opportunity to perform regularly. We are making giant strides at all levels only to fall short at the most important stage and why? Because too many clubs plan short-term and don't see the bigger picture. I'm lucky, I can just remember the time at Cas when overseas imports were limited and I was playing alongside English internationals - Cas born and bred. There's plenty of kids out there but we must give them genuine hope and an attainable goal.

Dad has just questioned how come the Aussies have just stuffed us and not one of them had so much as a bloody nose? He quotes the old days and then tries to justify it, I tell him the game's different nowadays. 'That's bollocks! It's only because that's how the Aussies want it played.' He replies.

I guess he has a point my dad.

2

In the Beginning

I was born on June 27th 1967 at Manygates hospital in Wakefield. My mum Mavis had met and courted my dad for a few years previous. I did not realise until reading Dad's book, that my first day on earth caused so much controversy in the Sampson family. He and Granddad having a major bust-up over his time keeping whilst I was snug as a bug in my cot with Mum keeping a watchful eye on me, oblivious to it all. I also didn't realise how I met my granddad Sampson for the first time on the promenade in Filey. There were quite a few revelations for me in Dad's book including some of his 'wild' adventures.

My earliest recollections are living at number 2, Temple View, Lofthouse. I have some good memories of our neighbours, Mr and Mrs Wrigley with whom I spent many hours some pushing my handmade wheelbarrow. Mr Wrigley had lovingly made me this mini barrow and although now long gone they were lovely people, as were the Grainger's, Joe and Margaret at number 3, again where I was always welcome, just as I was with Mr and Mrs Pinson at number 5 and the Rowley's at number 7. This three-storey row of five stone cottages overlooked southeast Leeds and Temple Newsom Hall hence the name Temple View.

1971 Brings my first recollections of Stanley, when we moved into the Ship Inn at Lee Moor where I grew up over the next fourteen years. Fourteen of the most glorious years any family could wish for, we had space galore and wanted for nothing. Jonathan my younger brother was only one year old and Rebecca didn't come along until 1974. The pub was situated at the top of Stanley in an area called Lee Moor. An area that Dad has since discovered our family have inhabited for over 250 years and ironically I could always see Temple View over the fields at the rear from my bedroom window.

The pub car park was at the rear and this fell away into swampy land, and every winter when the rains came this area would flood. I clearly remember Dad's constant battle with the rats who would invade the bin area. In the early hours he would poke my uncle Malc's .22 air rifle through his bedroom window then 'ping' and the rats would scarper. Dad would say he couldn't understand how they could run off so fast with so much lead in them night after night, but I suspect the 'ping' came from the pellets hitting the dustbin, which knowing Dad's condition after playing the disco and drinking a dozen lagers, well I suppose hitting the bin can be construed as a good shot.

As a young boy raised in a village pub, I suppose it was inevitable that I grew up with character traits formulated by the people, family, customers and pub life in which I was cocooned. When Mum and Dad were downstairs working I was king of the castle - upstairs that is - toys in abundance, access to TV, plenty of friends and acres of open space in the surrounding countryside to live out our fantasies.

Mum at this time rarely went to watch Dad playing so in my early years I saw little of the game of rugby. Dad was playing with Bramley at this time and a few years elapsed before I was allowed to attend on a regular basis. Mum would be working so Dad would leave me with Maureen Wolford and Sandra Austin whose husbands, Johnny

Wolford and Jack Austin, also played for Bramley. I was pals with Johnny's son Andy, we would play on the pitch at half-time and after the game had finished. This was my introduction to the game, all good fun, until I moved to Outwood Grange School, where in the newly formed Stanley Rangers Juniors I became serious. Living and breathing the worlds finest team game, I was hooked.

Dad was coaching at Stanley Rangers at this time, and he decided the club should have a junior section, so he asked me to recruit as many friends as possible. He would take us on cross-country jogs, intermittently pausing to fire a question on rules each time for a different boy, then after weeks of preparation a friendly game, then within a few more weeks a junior league was up and running. Alan Gibb, the former BARLA chairman was an early recruit, Alan had recently moved into the village and his youngest son Ian wanted to try rugby league. Steeped in rugby union from his Scottish homeland, Alan became a friend to Dad. Alan was a talented academic so his early assistance was invaluable to the formation of the juniors and of Stanley Rangers continued youth development. From the inaugural meeting at Shaw Cross back in the mid seventies, he converted and went on to be a magnificent servant to Stanley Rangers and then BARLA.

As for myself, I always had my bag at the ready for any occasion. At ten years old I got a game with the under fourteen's, at fourteen years a game with the open age second team which included a run out with Dad. Then by the time I was sixteen I got another run out with the open age first team at Sharlston. It was during that game that I was privileged to play with Johnny Wolford, I would have loved to play with him in the professional game, his hands and vision were fantastic.

As I grew I attained schoolboy honours and finally and inevitably I followed Dad to Castleford and then made my way through the ranks. First in the under seventeen's, then signing on as professional in June 1986 for the princely sum of £1,000. Sheffield made me an offer at the same time, for which I was flattered and grateful, but it was no contest really, although I have occasionally reflected how my career and achievements might have taken a different path if I'd elected to move to South Yorkshire.

In my first season with the Cas A-team we won the Yorkshire Cup against Hunslet at Bramley. Dad was coach and I received the man of the match award although he felt Johnny Milner at scrum-half, whom Dad had borrowed from Stanley, should have been the recipient. Then added to this I was voted A-team Player of the Year, obviously I was delighted but eager and hungry for more. I was training full-time now having given up my job as an apprentice fitter with Yorkshire Imperial Metals in Leeds. My time there was like going to gaol, everyday clocking in and out, Peter Fox was my training officer; a legendary coaching figure but the job simply did not feed my wanderlust spirit. Dad continued to encourage me and then came the bombshell, Malcolm Reilly took over the GB coaching job, full-time, and Dad was promoted to first team coach with John Kear and Mick Morgan as his assistants.

I remember Dad saying to me, 'because you're my son, to break into my first team you will have to excel a little bit more than the others. I'll not be accused of favouritism, nor you along with me'. Only pressure by John and Mick convinced Dad to open the season with me starting at prop against St Helen's at home, it was a brave decision and I was determined to repay his faith and John and Mick's. I don't think I let them down as I scored a try and we won, the press made a veritable meal both before the game and especially after. So far so good but little did I think then and had I been told I would have scoffed at the idea, that I would be still donning my Cas jersey in 2002.

John Kear who had been my coach in my first season went on to greater glory and has I'm sure had many trips to Shangri-La himself. And Mick Morgan like myself is still at Cas. He works tirelessly behind the scenes encouraging everyone with his effervescent infectious character, helping to lift us when we're down and chide us with some remark to keep our feet firmly on the ground if we think we are better than we really are. Characters at Castleford, both fans and staff are everywhere, and over the years I have fond memories of many such people; Darryl Van De Velde, John Joyner, Stuart Raper, Mal Reilly, Stuart 'Animal' Walker, Graham Steadman, Gary Mercer, Adrian Vowles, Dale Fritz, St John Ellis, Kevin Ward, Bob and Kevin Beardmore, Dennis Cackett, Jack Fulton, Keith 'Beefy' England, Martin Ketteridge, Johnny Walker and Dennis Hartley. I guess I've been lucky to work alongside some of the greats in the game. All in some way helped me become the player I am and influenced the man I have become.

3

Poor Old Oscar

All those people who know my dad, and no doubt those who have read his book, will realise he is a bit of a character. Although he will freely admit to making mistakes on his roller coaster life, I know he will argue that whatever he took on, he meant well.

One particular incident that gives an insight into his nature was the time my sister Rebecca woke up screaming and ran into Mum and Dad's bedroom shouting, 'something is under my bed!' Dad calmed her down and bleary eyed did a spot check but couldn't find anything so he returned Becky back to bed assuring her it must have been a dream. But the next night and the same event, Becky ran into Mum and Dad's bedroom again and this time she was insistent and petrified. 'There is something under my bed.' She moaned.

Becky's bedroom had previously been the dining area, which was partitioned off from the lounge. You had to go into the lounge to gain access by means of a sliding door that was always left slightly open. This particular night I lifted the bed and Dad began rummaging, pulling out Becky's toys and teddy bears, when suddenly he emerged holding the biggest hedgehog you have ever seen. I'll never forget his words. 'Now how the bloody hell did you get in?'

Mum was livid. 'It didn't climb the bloody stairs without help from someone, that's for sure. Get it out of here now; I'll have to fumigate everything.'

Dad gently handed the hedgehog to me. 'Take it down the stairs and let it out of the cellar son, so it can go into the fields.' Which I did. On returning mum had recovered from under Becky's bed a part eaten bag of jelly tots and an empty torn open packet of chocolate buttons.

Over a cup of tea at about two o'clock in the morning, Dad apologised to Mum and Becky and then explained. It seemed that almost three weeks previous on his legendary Thursday's down town; the taxi he arrived home in nearly ran over a hedgehog outside the pub. Dad in his infinite wisdom decided to name the spiky creature Oscar and brought him into the pub. An empty crisp box became an overnight shelter in the warmth of our upstairs lounge and Dad, contented that his good deed was done, so retired to bed.

Mum took over then. 'So the torn crisp box that I found next morning with Judy (our sheepish looking Blue Great Dane) must have been the one you put that hedgehog in. I thought she looked guilty, she probably wondered what was in it and tipped the box over.'

'Maybe she thought there were some hedgehog flavoured crisps.' I remember quipping.

When Dad arose the next morning, Mum had chastised the dog and put the box in the bin. Dad's recollection of anything regarding a hedgehog had vanished as soon as his head hit the pillow the previous night.

'Well it's bedtime,' exclaimed Dad, 'all's well that ends well.'

Next morning we found a squashed hedgehog in the middle of the road at the front of the pub, Dad always contended that it couldn't be Oscar because their were no signs of jelly tots or chocolate buttons. But I think there is a moral in this somewhere like, if you have enjoyed Dad's hospitality in the pub be extra careful crossing the road when leaving.

4

Early Days

In my first full season with Castleford, I played A-team rugby only, and although under Dad's watchful eye I knew I was improving, I still never got a sniff of being picked for the first team. Dean Mountain was the usual choice to fill in if a first team spot at prop was available and I occasionally felt that having my dad as coach was counter productive as I felt some of my performances warranted a chance. He contended I still had a lot to learn and to be patient, everyone kept saying that my time would come and when it did it would be up to me to grasp it and keep it.

During that season we won the Yorkshire Cup against Hunslet at Bramley's Mclaren Field, this match I know gave both my dad and myself great satisfaction. He had made his debut on the same pitch for Bramley against Leeds some twenty years earlier after leaving Wakefield. A few old friends were watching - people like Earnest Humphrey, himself a former player and director, and Frank and Ronnie the kit and grounds men, who all gave Dad a pat on the back - he loved it. As I said, we won the cup and to cap it all, I received the Man of the Match trophy. A good drink and a celebration was the order of the day but I must mention that it was a real team effort; I was playing alongside some quality players in a very consistent A-team. So consistent that on the narrowest of points difference we finished in second place in the Alliance League. Hull had to go to Wigan and win by a large margin to knock us off top spot, and judging on the formbook, I reckoned they had no chance. I remember a warm feeling of satisfaction that in my first season I had a Yorkshire Cup Winner's Medal and a Championship Medal in the bag. But then I'd forgotten the old proverb 'don't count your chickens before they've hatched'. Hull went to Wigan with a strong side and stuffed them and snatched the title from our grasp on points difference, I did however take some consolation at the club awards end of season ceremony by being awarded the Player of the Year. My first campaign had not been fruitless and no doubt the coaching I received in those early days has stood me in good stead in my career since.

In the summer of 1987 I trained harder than ever but then I noticed so were the rest of the squad, my dad had now taken over from Mal Reilly coaching the first team and many of the young players who had performed so well for Dad in the previous season were looking to kick on in to the senior squad. Also three Aussies joined Cas but this was after a pre-season match in Albi, a beautiful town in the southwest of France. Through our village club, Stanley Rangers, my dad had built up a friendly association with the Albi rugby league team. One of their officials, Monsieur Bernard Gariel, instigated a pre-season tournament with Cas and Halifax - Castleford being 1986 Wembley winners, Halifax 1987 winners. It was all expenses paid, Halifax agreed to take up the challenge and both teams flew to Toulouse where a coach picked us up and took us to our hotels. It was game on and both teams suddenly realised what was at stake when the trophy was unveiled, it stood fully three feet tall from base to lid and the travelling fans from both sides mingled amicably creating a carnival atmosphere throughout the town.

The match against Halifax took place in the Stade de Municipal; Dad had said that although it was a pre-season match, performances would be consideration for squad places so we went at the game at a furious pace. It was an evening kick-off but it was still very warm so subs and water were vital and after a close game we ran out winners. I'll remember John Joyner's words before that game forever. 'Come on lad's, let's win it for Sammy.' And we did.

Dad was a very proud man that night when he and John shared a drink after the game. The hospitality had been exceptional and although it's years on I'm still grateful to Bernard Gariel and all those who worked so hard to make it such an enjoyable trip and if I'm not mistaken that magnificent cup still adorns the Castleford trophy cabinet - Dad says he wouldn't know as he's never been invited in.

On our return from Albi, there was news of the three overseas players joining the club. Dad had been to Australia and signed Michael Beattie, a centre from St George, Johnny Fifita, a Tongan from the same club and Bobby Lindner, who was returning supposedly to give us a full season this time after doing a short stint the previous year. There was certainly an air of optimism about the place.

The previous season's first game against St Helen's on Sunday, August 30th 1987 at Castleford was my debut. For the record we won the match and the team that day was Castleford - David Roockley, David Plange, Tony Marchant, Grant Anderson, Giles Boothroyd, Shaun Irwin, Roy Southerwood, Alan Shillito, Kevin Beardmore, Dean Sampson, Keith England, Kevin Ward, John Joyner, Kenny Hill, Dean Mountain.

St Helen's - Veivers, Large, Loughhlin, Elia, McCormack, Batley,

Holding, Burke, Liptrot, Forber, Fieldhouse, Haggerty, Platt, Arkwright, Dwyer.

Referee - Mr Fred Lindop (Wakefield)

The half-time score was 8-8, and after full-time, 20-10 and the attendance for that day was 5,419.

During that season I got to start ten first team games under my dad and subbed thirteen times but I also doubled up with the A-team. Dad explained that stepping back down would do my development and confidence good. Then John Kear would reward me with a subs spot with the first team for a good display.

There were several eventful games that season for not only did we beat St Helens without an overseas player in the team, we repeated the feat against Wigan later in the season. I remember Dad making the point in his pre-match address. 'Some of you resent overseas players taking your positions, so go out and prove we can win without them.' We did just that, had a cracking start to the league campaign, and reached the Yorkshire Cup final against Bradford. The first game at Headingly ended all square with twelve points each. Then came the replay at Elland Road, which we were very unfortunate to lose. Suffering injuries to key players including Bob Lindner, the reshuffle affected us badly and after a disjointed second half display, we narrowly lost the game.

The Yorkshire cup defeat then proved to be a bit of a hangover on our league campaign, our form dipped and we lost our way. It was difficult to understand why because we then lacked any sort of consistency however, we managed to finish a creditable seventh in the league at the end of the season and even managed a revenge win against Leeds who had stuffed us earlier in the season 26-12 at

Wheldon Road.

Bob Lindner returned home before Christmas, once again, failing to fulfil the hopes of many Cas fans. He also slagged Dad off to the Castleford chairman, David Poulter, just as he had done about Mal Reilly the previous season. Dad quite philosophically put it in a nutshell when I asked him about his feelings on the subject. 'Look son, he was a gladiator who came to Rome but Spartacus he certainly wasn't!' Well I guess that puts things in perspective.

5

Dad Out - Darryl In

It was our last match of the 1987-88 season and the end of my first full term playing in the first team, we had finished seventh and had to play St Helens away in the play off. It was a fine day weather wise but we were well beaten on the pitch. I was pleased with my own performance, in fact I got another man of the match award but in the dressing room after the match, I did not comprehend the significance of the discussion in the doorway between my dad and the then chairman, David Poulter. It turned out Dad was being dismissed from his position as first team coach; I still wasn't aware when we boarded the bus for home or even when we disembarked at Cas bus station. Dad slipped quietly away while the rest of the team headed for the Jockey, I then followed Dad and he told me of his sacking.

As I drove home I was gutted, absolutely gutted, then the feeling turned to anger, 'bugger em' if my dad wasn't good enough to coach the team - which he certainly was in my eyes - then I wasn't willing to play for them. I was going to quit, to walk out, what did I owe them. I loved it at Cas but I'd played little more than a handful of games for the club and family loyalty comes first - before everything and anyone at any cost.

Dad told me to hang on and not make any rash decisions that I may regret at a later date, give myself time to come to terms with what had happened and not cut my nose off to spite my face. Again, Dad was full of wise words but I had difficulty seeing at the time, I was still livid with David Poulter for his actions after what we had achieved that season with the side we had. A Yorkshire Cup final, the British Coal nine-a-side final at Central Park where we were only beaten by home team Wigan, finishing seventh in the league and the club even made a profit that year due to some astute buying and selling of players. If Dad had got at his disposal the hundreds of thousands of pounds his successor got, then who knows what could have happened.

Personally I felt that a few of the players had let everyone down that season with their attitude and performances and none more so than Australian international Bob Lindner who Dad didn't even want but was told by David Poulter that he'd already signed him. I remember Bob breaking his nose in one game and was then out for about six or seven weeks. That's a hell of a long time for a broken nose and not what I call commitment to a club. Quite a few of the Cas player's were not very happy about this, especially when taking into consideration the money he was on.

But after cooling off, I decided to go the night after Dad's sacking to the annual general meeting at Castleford Civic Centre to listen to what the directors had to say. I decided it would be a chance to also defend Dad if anything untoward or defamatory was said about him as he wouldn't be there having been told not to attend by Mr Poulter. I also decided that night after considering Dad's advice and thinking how passionate the fans are about the team that I would stay at Castleford but I vowed I would never again trust David Poulter and my misgivings about him at this time were borne out later.

In the season of 1988-89, my progress can be noted by fourteen first team games plus thirteen appearances at sub. I also scored seven tries for the first team and although that was not bad, it wasn't as good as I'd been used to in the A-team. Still I was only twenty-one years old and starting to grow in both confidence and experience. Again, it had been a shared season between the first team and A-team and come the season end I was once more voted A-team Player of the Year.

I remember though that our new coach Darryl Van de Velde would drop me from the first team the minute I didn't perform at my best. Playing in the second team felt like a form of punishment being meted out on me, it just seemed at the time that if any of the more senior players had an indifferent game this didn't apply. I vividly recall expressing my doubts about my ability and future under this new man, but my dad thought I was playing reasonably well and slowly progressing. 'Have faith son, keep going and just remember this, you work for him, he is your boss so strive even harder to please him, no matter how unfair you feel he might be.'

That season we reached the Yorkshire Cup final again but were defeated 12-33 by Leeds at Elland Road, Gary Belcher, a nice bloke and great player, was one of our Aussie imports; alas, he was injured, missed the final, returned half his contract money and went home after only ten games.

During the latter part of this season there was considerable unrest in the camp with many of the younger players feeling insecure, believing Darryl had given up on them. Many felt their days were numbered, and they were right, the change in personnel was about to take on a dramatic turn.

Darryl's casualty list was a who's who of rugby at that time; John Kear, Barry Johnson, Kenny Hill, Roy Southernwood, Chris Chapman and Bob Beardmore. The twins Bob and Kevin had just enjoyed a bumper joint benefit season, collecting thirty-grand and I don't recall two nicer guys who played the game that were more deserving. When Dad was coaching, he could never tell them apart, I remember him once at Salford addressing Kevin in his pre-match talk as Bob and Kevin went along with it before spilling the beans. Dad was acutely embarrassed but saw the funny side and from then on it was a very relaxed dressing room. Anyway, Darryl's changes were fast and decisive but my shock was still to come. Before the start of the following season I was offered a contract of £4,200 for the year plus match payments, it wasn't a great contract but for a part-timer it was okay. Then I got the call into the office to see Darryl and David Poulter, they sat me down and told me that they wanted to sign Gary Divorty from Hull.

'No way.' I said.

'Well Hull have shown an interest in you and we'd like you to go as part payment for Gary.'

'You want what?'

'Don't worry,' said David Poulter, 'we are willing to give you a one-off £5,000 tax free payment to go to Hull.'

'But I don't want to go to Hull.'

'Well we would like you to, so why don't you go away, speak to Hull and think about it.'

I walked out of that office close to tears, the club didn't want me, the coach didn't want me, I'd come so far, through so much and now they were willing to give me more money to go than to stay, I struggled to come to terms with the irony of it all.

When Hull phoned me I spoke to the coach Brian Smith and he seemed really keen and enthusiastic. Hull were a pretty big team, the money was good - especially coupled with Cas's five grand, then out of the blue I was contacted by Wakefield coach David Topliss who had heard I was available and being a local Wakefield lad, would I be Interested in joining them. I thought no harm in having a chat, so I went along to Belle Vue and had a look round. They offered more money than either Cas or Hull did and also added a job and a car.

Things were looking up, Cas didn't want me but two other clubs did and I started to look on the positive side of things, telling all parties that I need a little time to think things over, then twenty-four hours later, my whole world came crashing down. First was a call from Brian Smith at Hull informing me that he had just signed Karl Harrison from Featherstone and they were no longer interested in me - CRASH! Then I phoned Stuart Farrar at Wakefield Trinity and told him I was ready to sign for my hometown club but he informed me that they had just signed a world class forward in New Zealander, Brent Todd and didn't want me now - BANG! The next day I went back to Cas and asked David Poulter that seeing as the Hull deal had fallen through, could I sign my original £4,200 a year deal, put every-thing behind me and just concentrate on playing rugby. No! I could sign a contract but a three-year one and for less money, take it or leave it - WALLOP! The rest as they say is history.

A hot and cold relationship is probably the best way I can describe my time with Darryl Van de Velde but in fairness to him, you couldn't question his preparation for a game. Now this opportunity I take to give you, the reader, an insight into his planning for each individual player before a big match. First, he would hand you your personal goals that he expected you to attain for a particular game. Second, he would ask you to hand him your intentions for that game. And third, you would receive a personal evaluation sheet after the match and before beginning work for the following weeks game.

After the Regal Trophy third round away at St Helens in December 1992, Darryl's evaluation sheet for my performance read:

Defence

Tackles completed: *33*

Missed tackles: *3*

Consecutive tackles: *0*

Attack

Mistakes/tackle: *0*

Number of drives: *17*

Mistakes in my own 22 metres: *1*

Penalties given and reason: *1 - holding*

Evaluation: *Good game Dean although more aggressive running needed. When you did you busted them open, however go straight. Defence sound with top tackle count. Total of 50 plays.*

Assessment out of 10: *8*

Result: *12 – 8 (won)*

I guess you had to hand it to Darryl – he was bloody thorough and certainly better prepared than any boy scout I know.

6

First Choice

Now I really was wound up, red wrath rising and so on. I was missing from the 1989-90 team photo call but not from the season, having played twenty-nine first team games, subbed only five, and scoring eight tries - one more than the previous season. As a team we won nothing but our new faces had slotted in well, while I faced every game with an 'I'll show them attitude', which was aimed specifically at Darryl and David Poulter. Overall, I had played well for Cas including a narrow 20-22 loss to New Zealand when Darryl praised my performance, but so far I had only under twenty-one honours and statements from all and sundry that I was on target for further representative rewards.

I was hungry for more when the season ended and I had my fingers crossed that maybe, just maybe, I would be given an opportunity to represent my country on tour. Dad warned me. 'Don't rely on media hype, they may have helped the odd player get chosen previously but Malcolm Reilly is his own man, he'll take who he feels comfortable with and he is too astute to be swayed by the press.'

Nevertheless, I was optimistic; I felt I had earned a call-up. However, my hopes were dashed when I attended a function at the Parkside Inn opposite Pontefract Racecourse. Malcolm was in attendance and he pulled me to one side. 'I won't be taking you Dean,

I already have a strong influx of youth in the pack so I'm taking Keith England and Paul Dixon to add experience.'

My heart sank, I was so disappointed and for days, I struggled to motivate myself about anything. Then I was contacted by an Aussie team, Mossman, who wanted me to play for them through the summer. What the hell, I thought, why not. I then discussed it with Darryl who said that if I was determined to go to Australia then he would have a word with Bob McCarthy, the coach of Gold Coast Seagulls, Queensland's new boys. I knew Bob was a legendary forward with the Kangaroos and I soon agreed terms - a car, accommodation, flights and a thousand dollars a game win, lose or draw. It was a ten-week contract in the sunshine of Queensland and I remember stepping off the plane jet lagged, but I pushed it to the back of my mind and that same afternoon I went water skiing with my new Seagulls teammates. Oh what a life, what a place, I was in Shangri-La but not for long though as next morning a ten kilometre beach run brought me back down to reality.

The morning after running my calf muscles were so sore I could hardly walk. I wasn't conditioned to beach work and had strained them, but fortunately a couple of days rest and treatment and I was raring to go again. I did some weight work both of those days and I know I impressed, but when you have worked out in a weight room as competitive as the one at Castleford with Mal Reilly, Kevin Ward and Keith England, well, I guess with a name like Sampson I think the Aussies expected my bench press to be impressive.

At this time, news was filtering through from England that Kevin Ward might be moving on to pastures new; I had mixed feelings about this as Kevin had been my hero. he was from Stanley, my village, and had played with my dad. I knew he wasn't over enamoured with Darryl but I reckoned it would be a big wrench for both Cas and Kev if he moved but I also wondered if this was to be my window of opportunity to shine. Maybe Cas felt that the money Kev would command was too good to refuse when taking his age into consideration. I had played alongside him that previous season, and Kevin was awesome, he was also a very fit thirty plus player who had the presence and ability to command respect from both his teammates and the opposition. I felt sure he still had plenty left in the tank, which proved correct as he went to St Helens and played another eighty-eight games, although his career was tragically ended with a horrific broken leg. Nevertheless, few players can boast legendary status with three clubs. As well as being a Cas and Saints all time great, Kevin guested with Manly in Sydney and he is still revered to this day for his man of the match performance in winning a Grand Final with them. I knew I would miss him when I went back to Castleford but then life goes on.

Bob McCarthy picked me for my first match in the reserves up against Wests on the first Saturday. Gary Divorty of Hull and Leeds had also joined the club and we both got to start, I recall it was hot and the papers quoted I had played an eye-catching thirty-five minutes. On the Wests team that day was Graham Mackay who went on to play with Leeds Rhinos, Bradford Bulls and is now centre for Hull. Also playing was Adrian Vowles, who later served at Castleford with such distinction before deserting us for the silver tails (only kidding Adrian).

After the first game, I was drafted onto the bench for the next first team match and then called up for the last twenty minutes. It was much tougher but really enjoyable.

Our next game was away at nearby rivals the mighty Brisbane

Broncos. I was promoted to start at prop second grade instead of the bench but although I knew Bob McCarthy and Malcolm Clift were not too keen to rush me, I was only over there for another ten weeks. Anyhow, I must have impressed at Brisbane because the following week I was named first choice prop to start against Balmain Tigers. Now at this time, I was aware that a pack containing Steve Roach, Ben Elias, Steve Edmed and Paul Sironen would get pretty hot and I don't mean just weather wise. Sledging was in abundance and tempers became frayed on occasions. In the end, we got stuffed 46-2, and my only consolation after being sin binned on five minutes was to take the Man of the Match award as well as topping the tackle count.

In reality, we were struggling as a team to cope with the big guns but for me, another three points rating against Manly meant I was extracting and learning as much as possible, I was even picked at second row for the second consecutive week with Ronnie Gibbs at sub. Who would have thought it back at Castleford as the season before Ronnie had starred in our pack!

I was having the time of my life; big games and big names, high profile media hype, sunshine and parties; although training and playing was always the number one priority. Then came our first win against Eastern Suburbs, this was a big lift to the whole club whose small squad was constantly decimated by injuries. Then the following week I started against Cronulla only to be flattened in an off the ball incident courtesy of Danny Lee's elbow. I was concussed and the referee reported Lee but he was later found to have no case to answer - I guess that's when I learned pommie bashing season in Sydney is in the month of July. In the end, I played nine first grade games in my short stint and Gary Divorty managed six. We both suffered with injuries but often carried knocks into games and I suppose it added a bit of irony when you consider that Cas were willing to swap me plus cash for Gary just twelve months earlier and give me more on top to go to Hull.

Coming to the end of my period in Australia, I couldn't wait to get home. I'd had a tremendous time at the Seagulls with new found friends playing superb rugby, a true Shangri-La. But now I was getting homesick and it started to play on my mind that I was approaching 100 appearances for Cas so I couldn't wait for the new season back in England. Some of the things I had gleaned from my all too brief sojourn were that collectively players were much fitter, but then the climate was a big plus, also referees were far and away more capable than ours and their league was much more organised and ruthless. But most of all it was the profile the game holds in the media in Australia. It's featured heavily in the newspapers, magazines, on TV and in advertising. Maybe the public down under have a greater appetite for the game or the Australian Rugby League have been more effective at marketing themselves but whatever, there doesn't seem to be the snobbery which is so often present in the British national press.

7

Darryl Out - JJ In

The 1990-91 season was especially satisfying for the club, Lee Crooks had signed in January and because of Darryl's pre season training, I noticed he was looking sharp. The squad seemed happy and very confident and our Aussie quota of Gary French, Jeff Hardy and Steve Larder quickly slotted into things. It was the third Yorkshire Cup final since I signed on and third time lucky for me. We were tipped to beat Wakefield but they had other thoughts, made us work very hard, and caused a few scares along the way before we emerged triumphant 11-8.

On a personal level, the season was especially satisfying for me; I swept the board receiving the clubs Player of the Year award. I had been Alliance Player in both 1986 and 1987, but receiving this award from my teammates gave me a real buzz. But the icing on the cake was still to come, Darryl presented me with the Coach's Player Award, I was ecstatic, I was in Shangri-La and make no mistake, I didn't come down for days, feeding myself on the euphoria with the knowledge and belief that the hard work and the pain had all been worth it.

Sun-tanned and feeling very fit, the season seemed to carry on where I'd left off at the end of the previous campaign and I achieved one of my long held ambitions to be a first choice player for Castleford and with thirty-four starts and only one at sub, I felt that's one monkey off my back.

Darryl continued to be a hard taskmaster and the selectors in their wisdom continued to ignore my claims for honours, but Darryl kept encouraging me as did Dad. 'Be patient, your time will come, you're still only twenty-two years old.' He told me.

Then the Aussies came to Castleford in November and with nineteen drives and thirty-two tackles plus plaudits all round I was satisfied that I could hack it with the best. We lost 28-12 but even the Aussies were commenting, 'what does this guy have to do to get in the GB team?' I was of course flattered but the Australian management can't be expected to pick our team even I knew that, anyhow the season passed and whilst no more silverware came into the cupboard, I knew I was playing with an ambitious coach and an ambitious club and I felt sure that there was more to come. These were thrilling times at Wheldon Road.

This year was also very special for John Joyner, he had deservedly been granted a twenty-year testimonial. To put JJ's career into perspective; well, my dad played against him in the early 1970s and then with him at Cas ten years later on. When you consider I was now playing alongside him in the early 1990s and he was still a class act, well, it's a credit to his stamina and ability, never mind his loyalty to Castleford. When my dad had been the Cas coach, JJ had been both his Team Captain and a loyal friend. I know Dad respects him, as do many others. His poise, balance and elegant running had given Cas fans over those years countless pleasure and even in the latter stages of his career after a move into the rough and tumble of the forwards, John was still highly rated, using his natural talents and eye for an opening to the full.

I now realise having amassed over 400 first grade games myself just what demands John had placed on both his mind and body to finish up with over 600 games. My dad keeps setting me new goals to aim for to keep me playing but that is one goal that will never ever be emulated. Dad will say, 'you'll regret it if Cas get to Wembley this year and you've packed in, you're a long time finished son'. It's getting to the stage where I'm expecting him to say, 'it's the dogs birthday next August, why don't you play until then son?' Well I heard that recently Jeff Grayshon was facing hip or knee replacements or both. Personally, I'd like to retire in one piece and stay that way.

John followed his great career by going into coaching, I hope to emulate him, it's a natural progression and it works with some of the big soccer clubs so maybe we should take a leaf out of their book.

As the season of 1991-92 arrived, Darryl once again changed some of the personnel. In came Graham 'Penguin' Bradley, Richie Blackmore and Tawera Nickau. I recall thinking this is as good a side as I have been involved with in my time so far. The blend seemed right and once again we won the Yorkshire Cup but this time against Bradford. A sweet revenge for 1987 when they beat us in a replay. We played out a convincing 28-6 victory and the man who took the honours was Graham Steadman with his searing runs when returning the ball. His two tries and four goals were a great contribution but it was also a superb team effort and I took great pleasure that seven of us were lads who had come through the production line - Martin 'Ketts' Ketteridge, Keith 'Beefy' England, 'Diesel' (me), Tony 'Casper' Smith, Graham 'Knacker Nuts' Southernwood, Neil 'Viking' Batty and Shaun 'Jim' Irwin. This time it was Tawera Nikau who hoisted the cup as Lee Crooks was injured. I was moved to number eight and Beefy came up to ten, while Shaun moved into the second row.

Before the game, some people reckoned we'd got no chance against Bradford but we came through in style, no doubt helped by a confidence boosting 38-26 win over Wigan only a few weeks before.

In the 1991-92 season we had lost five of the first ten league games, so winning the Yorkshire Cup gave us a real boost just when we needed it – in time for the Regal Trophy campaign. Our first road trip to Hull KR brought us a 22-10 victory but it was the draw for the second round, which captured the interest of our family. We were to play Doncaster at Wheldon Road and my dad was now their coach. Needless to say it caused a few raised eyebrows with the media but that was nothing compared to the atmosphere in the Sampson house-hold. As competitive as ever, Dad stated bluntly, 'we're up for it', and so it proved. Doncaster battled hard and after sixty minutes, we held a tenuous eight-point lead but fitness proved the difference and in the last quarter, we ran away with it to win 38-6. Dad shook Darryl's hand and wished him all the best. He later confided in me that we were good enough to go on and win it. I knew that was what Darryl wanted, oh he enjoyed winning the Yorkshire Cup but his ambition and a big lump of cash were driving him on for a major trophy, some-thing that all the clubs are involved in and this rubbed off on us as players.

Next up was a quarterfinal against archrivals Leeds but unfortunately we went down 24-4, and although I was happy with my game, it's small consolation, believe me, when as a team you have set your goal on winning. You win as a squad and you lose as a squad and you share the associated highs and lows.

On a personal basis, my goal at that time was to make the summer 1992 tour to New Zealand and New Guinea so I worked hard at maintaining my form. Competition for places in the Cas team was very intense but even so I still managed thirty first team appearances although eleven of them were as sub which disappointed me, although in fairness I was called to perform for a fair stint in every game.

We maintained our league form throughout the season and achieved a very creditable third place. We were one of the best teams of the division, spirits were high and confidence spread throughout the squad as we moved towards the semi-final of the Challenge Cup. Now this would have to go down as the one of the biggest games in my career, and the tension was heightened by the fact that our opponents, Hull, had been a cup bogey side to Cas. But not this year, we won 8-4 in a torrid encounter and the prize, Wigan at Wembley.

Darryl had moved Graham Bradley into the second row after bringing him over as a centre, which had further intensified competition for places in the pack. Wigan were favourites for victory after thrashing Bradford 71-10 in the other semi-final and Darryl's attitude towards me was making me even more nervous that I might not make the squad. My fears were further endorsed when after playing against Halifax on the Sunday, he ordered me and me alone from that team to turn out the next night at Warrington for the second team. I thought it was outrageous but dutifully complied, but fate works in strange and cruel ways. On that Monday night, I broke the fifth metacarpal in my left hand in five places - goodbye to any dreams of Wembley. My thoughts went out to my uncle Malcolm as I now knew how he felt when with Wakefield Trinity in 1960, having achieved a semi-final win at Warrington - he was robbed of his first Wembley appearance on a similar Monday night, except his was a car crash but like me an injury to the left hand. Nothing could console me; my inner pent up anger with Darryl was tearing me apart. The next day I visited the hospital, and to Castleford's credit, they pulled out all the stops. The surgeon advised an operation and to have a plate inserted, but with Wembley just two weeks away he said it would be nip and tuck however with painkilling injections I might just make it. I returned to the club a little more optimistic buoyed by the surgeon's encouragement. 'You can come back after Wembley and I'll take the plate out.' Were his parting words. This optimism was not to last long as Darryl took me to one side and explained I would have to prove my fitness by playing again before Wembley and if I did, I must do all the preparatory training that the others do and not once must I show a sign of pain. I looked at the fixture list and agreed to be available - I was not giving up my Wembley jumper without a fight even though I knew deep down that the best I could probably hope for would be number fifteen, forward sub.

With my hand heavily strapped and padded after a painkiller, I played and Darryl named me in the squad. I've always wondered, probably without foundation, did he want me to make it or did he hope I'd fail. John Joyner would have taken my subs shirt had I not had the necessary resolve, and in retrospect I prefer to think of it as Darryl using mind games with me to build my mental toughness and encourage fighting motivation.

Walking out at Wembley was a very special occasion. I had been well prepared by both Dad, who was assistant to Mal Reilly in 1986 and my uncle Malcolm who scored a try there for Wakefield when they beat Wigan in the 1963 final. Dad advised me. 'Dean, absorb the passion and spectacle of the occasion.' Whilst Uncle Malcolm said. 'We were the underdogs in 1963 against Wigan and that's an advantage.' Well I took the advice and I can still taste the electric atmosphere today. And even though we lost to a magnificent Wigan, the memory of those wonderful fans who for eighty minutes had bayed for the blood of the other team, sportingly applauded both the victors and the vanquished. I don't believe the 28-12 score line was a true reflection of the game but probably the differentiating factor was the pace of Martin Offiah who scored two tries out of nothing.

I promised myself I would return one day to that magnificent stadium, I also promised that we would one day exact sweet revenge on the mighty Wigan. It was their fifth Wembley victory on the trot and Castleford's first Wembley defeat on their fifth visit.

After the highs and lows, I joined my teammates on our end of season trip to Magaluf. We had earned our holiday after finishing third in the league table, Wembley runners-up and winning the Yorkshire Cup and I am sure none of the Cas fans would begrudge us letting off some steam for a week. When I returned, I headed off for a holiday with my girlfriend Lorraine. We jetted to Cyprus, which included a romantic trip to see the Pyramids in Egypt and a diamond factory in Israel and a subsequent engagement ring! Once again I had been overlooked for the tour and was beginning to believe it would never happen.

When I returned my priority was to start training again as the last three weeks had taken their toll; boozing, dancing, eating and sun bathing might give you an outside appearance of well being, but looks can be deceiving. Then shortly after getting back my dad called me on the phone. 'Will you pop up and see me son?' He casually asked. He was sat at his desk in Samson's, our pub in Stanley, I climbed the stairs and we met. 'Hi son, I've just had a phone call from Rugby League Headquarters, they want you to fly out to New Zealand immediately to join the tour party.'

'You've got to be joking dad.'

'No son, you had better get cracking.'

Before I knew it I was on a plane for New Zealand with instructions where to join the tourists, but my arrival was soon tinged with disappointment when I realised I was to play for the midweek squad. A great set of lads I recall and I was a very proud man when I pulled on my Great Britain jumper against both Canterbury and Auckland. They were two very tough games, but we achieved a win and a draw - hard earned but a great experience.

This had been a very eventful year all round and whilst I hadn't been selected for the big international games, I still took satisfaction from taking the next step in my career.

On returning to Cas, the whispers were that this was to be Darryl's final season. Knowing Darryl, he would want to go out all guns blazing; however, it was not to be. It was pretty much the status quo for me, twenty-one starts and thirteen subs compared with nineteen and eleven in my previous season. But overall 1992-93 turned out to be pretty much a damp squib compared with the excitement of the previous campaign. In the Challenge Cup, we lost narrowly 12-8 at Leeds and our league form was inconsistent throughout, then before the end of the season, Darryl announced officially that he was heading back home to take over at Queensland Crushers. I had mixed feelings at the news, I hadn't always seen eye to eye with Darryl but he had improved me as both a player and a man, I just wondered if I would have improved as much under someone else, but that I'll never know. Everyone wished him well for the future but then the news that John Joyner was taking over the reins was greeted with enthusiasm all round.

Featherstone had tried to sign me during the summer and a very persuasive Steve Martin almost convinced me but I still had something to prove not only to myself but also to Cas. I'd been first choice forward before but since the awesome Lee Crooks had joined the squad I'd been pushed back a bit, however I vowed I would be first choice again. Also in the summer I had got married and I think that contributed to me wanting to keep a bit of stability in my playing career.

Our wedding day was June 5th, a beautiful summer Saturday at Stanley church. My mother-in-law to be had managed through the Sun newspaper to acquire the services of photographer Arthur Edwards, Princess Diana's favourite snapper. We were seriously chuffed that he had travelled so far just for us and he took some memorable snaps. Arthur quipped in the Sun when the photo and caption appeared: 'They were all lovely people, salt of the earth.' I recall my dad proudly agreeing. 'How true.'

Back at the club, some more new faces were arriving and I was particularly excited about Tony Kemp teaming up with Richie Blackmore. JJ had questioned Dad about Tony's credentials at my wedding as my dad had coached Tony at Doncaster. He quite rightly gave Tony a glowing CV and along with Richard Russell and Ian Smales, we reckoned our team had plenty of flair. Personally, I was optimistic; I felt I had a part to play in this team, which for me endorsed my decision to stay. I couldn't wait for the season to come and a cracking season it turned out to be. John Joyner was awarded Coach of the Year, which was a well-deserved accolade. His achievement was to inspire, coach and blend the squad and he finally laid the Wigan ghost to rest.

The Regal Trophy final was just a few short months into John's reign, Cas not only beat Wigan 33-2 but it was the biggest margin of defeat they had ever suffered in eighty-seven major finals. However, although elated by the result, I was disappointed to start on the bench and only got on the field towards the end of the game. I struggled to really savour the occasion because of my limited involvement and afterwards I made a greater resolve to get a bigger slice of the action in the team. I was finding playing alongside Tony Kemp inspirational, he was easy to read and with him and Tawera spraying passes, plus prompting from Crooksie, well, I felt I was making progress.

Wigan gained revenge for the Regal Trophy final very quickly, beating us in the semi-final of the Challenge Cup, but glory came knocking on our door in the semi-final of the Stones Premiership Playoffs. We had to beat Bradford to go to Old Trafford and we did, 24-16. They were gutted and our prize for the victory was another meeting with Wigan. We went into the match confident in the knowledge that we had already beaten them to one trophy so we reckoned we could do it again. Now this Premiership final of 1994 sticks in my mind for quite a few reasons, not only was it at Old Trafford - another thing I can tell my kids - but it was my first time in the starting line-up, open side front row in a major final. I suppose at the time, not making the start for the regal trophy of that year still smarted and so I was out to make amends.

Arriving at our hotel on Salford Quays early Saturday afternoon, we were given the chance to have a look around the theatre of dreams and to walk on the hallowed turf, something not many people get to do believe me as the ground staff would kill before see anyone desecrate their holy carpet. As the players neared the outside of the penalty area a rugby ball appeared as if by magic onto the field of play. Tony Morrison a second rower from the Manchester area was jumping up and down in the nets looking like Swinton's answer to Peter

Schmeichel. 'Somebody take a shot then.' He bellowed. 'Come on; put one past me if you can.'

The ball bounced end over end fully thirty metres out from where Tony stood, crouched in a keepers stance ready to pounce like an agile cat, that was until the ball passed the path of Graham Steadman who unleashed a right foot volley that David Beckham would have been proud of. The ball rocketed passed several players heads on an arcing trajectory into the top right hand corner of the net. Poor Tony stood rooted to the spot, his head looking over his left shoulder his eyes fixed upon the mitre multiplex sat nestled in the back of the net. He hadn't moved an inch had our Tony, his reflexes were more like a corpse than a cat. The stunned silence that encompassed the whole of our party was only broken by Steady's voice. 'Not bad eh, for me bad leg?' There was laughter all around as Tony protested that he hadn't been ready and he couldn't see the ball because everyone was in the way, but we were having none of it. Castleford Tigers 1, Manchester United 0. Steady left the field with an extra skip in his step and a broad grin on his face whilst Tony added that he only had his trainers on and he would have slipped if he'd tried to save the ball. As the last of the players left the pitch, an old feller who was tending to the outfield with a fork slyly commented. 'Well lads that's probably the best goal never to be seen at Old Trafford.' Tony could still be heard complaining at the back of the bus on the return journey to the hotel.

Back at the hotel I passed a very sheepish looking Chris Smith, our young winger. Chris was sporting a very badly swollen hand and the bruising was just beginning to come out, the youngster was on his way to see the physio. The official story was that Chris had been out walking his dog that morning before meeting up with the rest of the team at lunchtime. Apparently, while out on a path in the countryside Chris had been the victim of a group of mischievous youngsters who were out with an air rifle taking pot shots at the local wildlife and Chris must have come into this category in the eyes of these mini snipers. The morning's tale was relayed throughout the journey and well into the afternoon, Chris protesting that these little mischief makers were harmless, we didn't need to involve the police and they had run off anyway – which was surprising as he was the fastest in the team and could easily have caught them. Then the coaching staff and some of the players started to get suspicious when it became apparent that the team joker, Ian 'Singe' St John Ellis, seemed to know so much about the events, but all involved were sticking to the script like glue. Anyway, Chris managed to play but then afterwards the real story came out. What had really happened was Singe had purchased a new air pistol and was showing it off to several players that morning. He was demonstrating his prowess as a marksman and managed to get Chris to hold a target - a matchbox - between thumb and forefinger at a distance of several metres. Now this is where the story differs depending on who you listen to. Chris said, 'Singe was just a crap shot', whilst Singe was of the belief that, 'the sights were out and anyway, Chris didn't hold the matchbox still'. Well they say front rowers are dumb, but these two must have been the thickest wingers in the game!

Sunday came and we consumed a hearty breakfast with relish, nerves had never been a problem for me, no drum banging, horn blowing or flag waving. The build up for me consists of quiet reflection on past good performances to build my confidence and every now and again, I remind myself of my role and input for the forthcoming game. It was a final yes, but my preparation was no different from any other game I played in.

The morning seemed to drag on, the pre-match meeting attended, the walk completed, lunch finished off, then 1.15 pm, time to board the bus. The journey was short and full of exited chatter. As we neared Old Trafford there seemed to be a sea of cherry and white, Wigan fans everywhere with little pockets of Castleford black and amber dotted around. The game was a double header with London and Workington contesting the Division One final, this game was just about to kick-off so when we jumped off the bus, a few of us dumped our bags in the changing room and went out to catch a little of the atmosphere. Singe was particularly interested as he was currently joint top try scorer with London's Mark Johnson so whichever of them scored most that day would be crowned Rugby League's number one try scorer for the 1993-94 season. Singe was confident, Singe was always confident, there was nothing Singe couldn't or hadn't done and he often regaled us with his stories of daring and danger, each one outdoing the last. Come to think of it, I could probably write a book just about the escapades of Ian St John Ellis.

Back inside I put my kit on, donned my boots and was ready to go. I remember when we went out to do our pre match warm-up that the Workington fans booed, hissed and hurled abuse at us. They were pretty pissed off as they saw us as being disrespectful to their team, who were about to collect the Division One Premiership Trophy and here we were running about in front of their end of the ground. I guess looking back, I understand why they were so upset, they don't win many times up in Cumbria so for us to be seen to be taking the edge off it was probably a bit hard to accept, but we had nowhere else to warm up, so tough.

Leaving the changing rooms to stand in the tunnel I suddenly had this rush to my brain, I'm not sure what it was but the hairs on the back of my neck stood on end, my teeth ground together and I was overcome with a feeling of energy surging through my body. Today was going to be a day to remember, I thought. If only I'd known.

As we ran out on to the pitch, the noise was deafening, the next thing we were kicking off to Wigan. Phil Clarke brought that first ball back and I went to hit him hard. He raised his arm as several of my fellow defenders converged upon him, I swung my right arm whack! That was sweet, that would have had to hurt. Ouch! That did hurt - my hand was throbbing. Several minutes passed before we received a penalty and the physio was able to get to me. 'You OK?' Bernie asked.

'No, I think my thumbs gone.' I replied

'Do you want it strapping then?' No sympathy, no concern, just get on with the job, that was our Bernie, a great physio but not one to freely hand out the TLC.

Ten minutes in and I latched onto a beautiful inside ball from Steady. I was travelling at speed and not too far out then down I went, CRASH!, BANG!, WALLOP!, I was over for a try, first blood to the Tigers. All season Shaun Edwards and Martin Offiah had done this post try celebration where they stood facing each other and nodded their heads repeatedly at each other with their hands placed on their hips. To them it probably seemed great, but to everyone else outside Wigan it was bloody annoying, to be honest there was probably a bit of jealousy involved as they scored about seventy tries between them that year, so they were at it all the time. Well not being one to miss an opportunity to take the piss, I was straight to my feet, faced my teammate and we started nodding like a couple of demented Status Quo fans. The Wigan boys weren't too impressed, but hey, they'd been the biggest piss takers in the game.

We turned around for the second half. My hand was easing up, it had been on fire during the interval but I'd had something to ease the pain. Cas were losing and Wigan had the ascendancy at this point. Then Kelvin Skerrett, the Wigan prop had a penalty against him for disputing a decision. We took a quick kick into touch and I was first up to take the drive. Now at this point anyone who saw the match will have an opinion on what happened next, was it deliberate or was it an accident? The Wigan fans would say it was deliberate, the Castleford fans would say they didn't give a toss, he'd given out enough in his time and he'd finally got his comeuppance. Well I'll tell you the truth. I received the ball at pace and in that instant in my peripheral vision I just picked out a figure in cherry and white hurtling towards me, my first reaction was to defend myself, but I was too slow and the player made impact with my forearm. I broke the attempted tackle but was then met by a wall of Wigan defenders. The tacklers untangled themselves and retreated the ten metres but as I reclaimed my feet to play the ball there was a commotion over my right shoulder. I looked behind and saw Wigan's prop Kelvin Skerrett, blood coming from his mouth, being escorted from the field by the Wigan physio. I thought shit that must have been Kelvin who I collided with. He was saying something but I couldn't understand a word so I just shrugged my shoulders and turned back to play the ball. But the referee had stopped play and was consulting with the linesmen and the Wigan players had by this time got it about between themselves that I had busted Kelvin's jaw with my elbow and all manner of threats were being thrust in my direction.

Now at this time, my granddad and his wife Mabel were watching the game in a pub in Cumbria. The pub was full of Wigan fans who were cheering their team on quite exuberantly then Granddad went to the toilet just before the incident happened. When he came back, he asked my grandma what all the commotion was about. 'Have Cas scored?'

'No your Dean's just smashed that Wigan lads jaw and they're gunning for his blood, so keep your mouth shut 'cos if they find out who we are they'll lynch us.'

Finally the referee restarted play and it was Andy Hay, our young back rower who had the pleasure of taking the next drive, the Wigan defence was 'enthusiastic' to say the least. Then as Nathan Sykes lined up for the third drive, I thought to myself they're after me so why should I let them wait, lets get it over sooner than later. So I nipped in front of Nathan and took the ball as the Wigan pack came in to get a piece of me. Watching the video later, boy was I lucky; I ducked just in time as Cowie's elbow just missed knocking me into next week. But by taking that drive so early after the incident and giving the Wigan boys, what they thought was an opportunity to exact revenge for a fallen team mate, well it seemed to settle things down and the game soon returned to normal.

In the end we lost by four points, I collected my losers medal and trudged off to the changing rooms. I was sat there with my right hand packed in ice, having just been informed that I'd probably broken my thumb, with my runners-up medal beside me when I was told by one of the directors that Wigan were citing me over the Kelvin Skerrett incident, turned out he had a badly broken jaw. Well bugger them I said to myself, I'm off to Benidorm tomorrow on our end of season trip and nothing's going to spoil that, not even Jack Robinson the Wigan director, who was citing me.

So for all those fans who wanted to sate their appetite for blood-letting between Kelvin and me, I'm sorry it was an instinctive protective action during the split second of a collision. I didn't mean to break Kelvin's jaw and I hope one day we can enjoy a drink together and reminisce, but only time will tell.

The disciplinary panel took a dim view and meted out their version of justice, but the video can and does lie on occasions and I know my conscience is clear.

8

The Sting

It probably happens to everyone at sometime in their lives in some form or another and this one was a classic, call it a learning curve, I do, that way I can live with it.

It was November 1992 and Dad and I were in our pub, Samson's, playing pool with a couple of the regulars, when the Tap Room door opened and a chap walked in asking for the governor. Dad approached him and made himself known and suddenly they were sat in deep conversation. It seemed this bloke had quoted the name of one of Dads friends from Kippax as a reference and he had some boxes of spirits for sale - all the real McCoy and legit, he assured us. Well Dad ordered a box of whisky, so the bloke added. 'If you buy two boxes, I'll add a couple of litre and a half bottles of Martini. So over the next five minutes Dad made up an order with him and he totted the cost on a note pad. 'That's £446 altogether, if it's cash I'll knock the forty-six quid off and we can call it a straight £400. Where can we unload them?'

Dad jumped up to his feet. 'Meet me at the back door.' He replied.

When Dad opened the back door, the chap stepped inside. 'My mate's just turning the van around so we can unload out of the back. He'll be here in a minute.'

Dad was now counting a bundle of tenners from his pocket. 'Dean,

nip upstairs and get me another hundred quid off your mum please.'
I was back in a flash thinking Christmas had come early - we were
sure to make a few quid out of this. The bloke was making a receipt
out for Dad as I approached them both at the bottom of the stairs. I
held out the money to Dad but this chap said. 'Can I check that, your
dad's just double checking the other three hundred?' He took the
hundred off me, turned to Dad and spoke as he flicked through the
cash. 'Ten tenners - a hundred, look do you mind if I put this in my
back pocket, I split fifty-fifty with my driver, but it's my gear so I'll tell
him I only sold it for three hundred?'

Dad shrugged his shoulders. 'Whatever.' He replied.

At this the chap opened the door and peered out into the car park.
'My mate's here with the van, where do you want it dropping?'

'In here - Dean go through and open the back cellar doors will
you?'

As I turned to go through to the cellar, the bloke turned back
towards Dad and offered him the receipt. Dad handed him the three
hundred quid and both stepped outside. But when I came to the door
I was just in time to see this guy sprinting down the car park, he leapt
the wall and dived into an awaiting car, the back door already opened,
the car then sped off. I jumped in my car and gave chase but all to no
avail, they had vanished into thin air so I returned to the pub mad as
hell. Dad was waiting for me with a half bemused look on his face,
which then broke into a wry smile. He then said. 'That guy deserves
a medal for valour, I take my hat off to him - can you imagine what
we would have done to him in the back entrance had we cottoned on
earlier?'

'We couldn't even call the police in case the brewery found out and
anyway we would have been the laughing stock of Wood Street police

station if we had.

'Put it down to experience son.' Dad said. I did.

9

Value for Money

Being the son of a publican in a small village like Stanley, I sometimes reflect on the characters propping up the bar and wonder if the same is happening throughout the Western World. I suppose the Ship Inn on Lee Moor Road could be likened to say a bar in the Australian Outback, or an establishment off Wall Street in New York or even (probably tenuously) an Amsterdam coffee shop – all places to relax, pass the time of day and enjoy a bit of banter with your mates.

During some of the more peaceful opening hours, I would volunteer to mind the bar, giving a welcome respite to Mum and Dad and it was during such times that I realised the mischievous comical nature of my granddad and his drinking buddy, old Mr Scott. Every lunchtime they would spend a leisurely couple of hours quaffing their pints of foaming ale and putting the world to right. Now on this particular occasion our two local council representatives, who were also regulars, were propping up the bar. 'Two halves of mild please my man.' And when they had consumed two each, after some polite banter these two dapper little fellows, neither standing much above five foot, bid good day to all. 'Bye George and Earnest,' and turning to me, 'give our regards to your mum and dad young sir.'

I'll do that Harold, no I won't forget Jim.' I replied.

Both simultaneously doffed their trilbies and waddled up the lane like a couple of miniature Laurel and Hardies. I turned to my grand-dad and asked. 'What do they do for a living and why is he known as "America Jim?"'

'Well they're both village elected councillors. Harold works for the council on the bin's, Jim doesn't work and I don't think he ever has, as for him being called America, that's not a name used in public but it is one that he earned many years ago when he was first elected. The council were short of money and asked for suggestions on how to raise some so Jim volunteered; he said he would convert his tin bath into a boat and do a sponsored sail to America hence the name America Jim. When he asked the council if they would be the first to sponsor, a wag stood up at the back of the chamber and offered his loofer and I know it's true because my mate Harold Colley told me and he was in the chamber at the time.' Said Granddad.

I was already laughing as I watched them disappear from view, then old Scotty interjected. 'It's right Dean and what about that time when the council announced it were gonna' put a gondola on lake in Wakefield Park and Harold stood up in chamber an suggested "Mr Chairman, I propose you put two on so they can breed."'

Old deaf Alf was chuckling in his chair and nodding approval, he adjusted his hearing aid to full reception as he added his two-penny worth to the banter. 'Hey George what about the time Jim came in the pub one Friday night, I remember somebody asked him what he was going to do about the one hundred and twenty thousand pound deficit announced that morning in the Wakey Express. And Jim answered him like a shot, "I'm going to insist we build an old people's home in Stanley with it, yes that's what we will have."'

The pubs half a dozen or so customers were now at mischievous full throttle and my sides were getting sore such was the banter. Old

Tom Field was bending vigorously up and down having risen from his chair his right arm hanging limply toward the floor. 'Is he all right Granddad?' I asked.

'Yes lad he's just pumping blood round, he'll be alright, not to worry.'

Just then the postman walked through the front door. 'Pint of shandy young Sammy, I'm gagging.' He bellowed. 'What's all the jollity?' He then asked.

'Just banter Willie, just banter,' replied Granddad. Then Granddad said. 'What do we know Willie, owt or nowt?'

'Nowt George, nowt, oh I tell a lie, I saw Dickie Linnett pushing a handcart up Bottomboat Hill. Been evicted he has.'

Old Tom chimed in. 'Not been paying his rent I hear.'

'Yes I wouldn't pay rent for that drafty old slum.' Willie replied. 'I was down there last week, the letterbox wouldn't open so I shoved his gas bill under the door three times, and three times it blew back out. Pip Matthews used to live there an he reckoned it were a dump.'

'Well Pip left there because of bugs.' Granddad muttered.

Willie piped up. 'I told Dickie this morning George, I said he had a team on his handcart that could beat owt in village!'

At this time I decided I needed to visit the loo, I made my way around the bar and as I entered I held the loo door for a quiet old man who I had never seen before that morning. He thanked me and as we both stood at the stalls he mentioned that he had enjoyed himself no end and that he had walked from Thorpe and was going to Stanley Post Office to cash his pension. But because of staying at the pub the Post Office had shut until two o' clock and he had spent up. Well I had served him about five pints that day and he seemed a nice enough old bloke so I said. 'Well if you want to stay, I'll lend you a tenner, and then you can bob back later on when you've been and drawn out your pension.'

'Oh that's very kind young man, will you still be open?'

'Oh yes, Granddad and his friends will be playing dominoes soon.' I lent him a tenner and sped back behind the bar to a chorus of 'come on young Sammy we're gagging'.

Well the banter continued for a couple of hours but gradually the customers dispersed and went about their daily business. The domino school broke up and myself and Granddad stood looking out of the window as the old stranger made his way up the hill and over the rise. I mentioned to Granddad about lending him the tenner. Granddad sighed and said. 'Did you say cheerio to him?'

'Yes of course I did.' I replied, as I returned my gaze to the window to watch a slowly disappearing torso and trilby hat. Granddad leaned over and whispered. 'Well young man I reckon you can say cheerio to that tenner as well.'

I never saw that stranger again but what the hell, the entertainment I had that afternoon playing landlord was worth every penny of Dads tenner.

10

Size Isn't Everything

I've been involved in a number of on field incidents but probably the daftest and most embarrassing didn't happen in a first team game but on a Saturday afternoon at Featherstone in the A-team. The match hadn't been particularly dirty but several incidents had warranted the referee's attention and after one, the ref awarded a scrum ten metres in from touch on the halfway line. Tempers were running a little high and as the scrum went down – BANG! To this day I don't know who threw that first punch but all hell broke loose with every player running from all over the field to put there two-penny worth in. Now I was suffering from a bad shoulder and as this was my first game back, the physio had furnished me with a shoulder harness, a contraption that connected your upper arms to your chest with short straps. The purpose of this being so you couldn't raise your arms too high or too far from your body so restricting your movement, which meant less chance of an injury again.

Back to the fight - as I broke from the scrum I came face-to-face with the short side winger, a well built but not too big coloured lad who I later discovered was called Barry Drummond. Now, retaliate first was always my motto so I sent a thundering right cross towards Barry's head which stopped suddenly - inches from it's target. Shit the harness. Too late - BOOM, BOOM, BOOM. What the fuck! I thought to myself as I stepped back quickly putting my hand to my face, I had the unmistakable warm sticky feeling of blood, on my hand. Well now I was really pissed off, he'd caught me with three stinging punches, the harness meant I couldn't hit back so I leapt forward thinking if I just get a hold and get close I can use my head. BANG, BANG, BANG I'd used my head all right to stop three more beauties from Barry. So I made a diplomatic retreat out of Barry's reach to study my options. Who was I kidding? What options did I have with a cut and swollen lip, a cut eye and a busted nose. I couldn't punch due to the harness, I couldn't get close enough to use my head as he was too quick, thankfully the shrill of the referee's whistle and the intervention of a touch judge saved Barry from giving me a real good hiding.

The boys had a good laugh at my expense after the game - a front rower getting a pasting from a winger! The next day the first teams were playing at Wheldon Road and I was in the bar about an hour before kick off when I spotted Barry coming toward me. Right, I thought, no harness on, close quarters; don't get caught by those fast hands. To my surprise Barry stuck out his hand, smiled, and said. 'Sorry about yesterday, I was out of order.'

'No problem, I came at you first, you just beat me to it.' As we got talking, it turned out Barry had just joined Featherstone after a successful career as a Golden Gloves amateur boxing champion. I certainly know how to pick them, I thought to myself. To this day whenever I see Barry, I remind him of the day a winger beat the crap out of a front rower. It just goes to show that size isn't everything...

11

A Rugby Village at War

In 1985 our family upped anchor and left our pub, the Ship at Lee Moor, to move half-a-mile down the road to the Travellers. My mum and dad had decided a more traditional pub would be easier to run which in turn would allow Dad more time for coaching at Cas. The soccer team who for many years had played under the Trav's banner because it was the Tetley Sunday league would move from the Ship into custom-built new dressing rooms at the Travellers, but Stanley Rangers rugby league team was to stay at the Ship. This was beneficial because of previous problems with over crowding in the changing rooms, and was generally welcomed by all the players.

The new landlord of the Ship was a bloke called Alan McCurrie, like Dad a man steeped in rugby league. Alas, as in many cases in the pub business, a change of landlord can bring in unforeseen problems and if not addressed properly things can begin to go downhill very quickly. Alan supported the Stanley Rangers teams, his son Steve played with the juniors. But for Alan and his family the pub business didn't work out and in 1986 they decided to move to pastures new and while the junior section prospered the open age team began to go into rapid decline.

Finally, after persistent failure to fulfil fixtures the first team disbanded. Long serving people, now administrators, such as Peter

Ashton, Ben Sellers, Ian Harris, Les Starkey, all ex-players who had given yeoman service for many years were helpless to halt the decline. Summer came and those in the village who were steeped in Stanley Rangers rugby were heartbroken until Ben Sellers came and had a chat with Dad. 'I think with your help David we could restructure the open age in time for the following season...'

By this time Dad's contract with Cas had not been renewed so he decided to turn out for the team and went into full training. Long lost players rejoined, new blood was welcomed. I trained whenever I could to encourage others and actively cajoled people to help. Ben Sellers, Dad and Peter Ashton brought in former chairman and stalwart, Brian Rowley, and a committee was formed. Then Dad donated the cost of a strip and the first season's insurance money, and with Ben, met the committee of the remaining juniors. They proposed that the seniors would operate from the Trav's but all monies raised would be forwarded to the Ship committee thus keeping the village rugby team under one banner, Stanley Rangers RLFC. It wasn't the perfect solution but if everyone pulled together it could work. The Trav's dressing rooms were available for Saturday rugby and Sunday morning football, and would alleviate the ever-increasing pressure on the facilities at the Ship.

Unfortunately at this stage, village politics reared its ugly head and whispers started going round that both the open age and junior teams should be run from the Ship, I know Dad was a bit upset and he put it down to a couple of the committee members. Then Dad and Ben were summoned to a meeting before the full committee. They stated they wanted both operations running from one pub, but Dad and Ben replied that it wouldn't be an ideal scenario as neither had sufficient dressing accommodation to cope, they also pointed out that the committee had allowed the open age team to disband once already. To which the committee said that if the open age team was to use the Travellers then the junior team must also move but Dad explained that that would not work either because of the lack of space. Well unfortunately the matter descended into an argument which resulted in Ben Sellars and my dad being sacked from the team.

Ben was disgusted, he told me. 'Your dad's invested into the lads who had nothing and asked for nothing, he's trained and played at forty-four years old, taken the team to a championship final play-off and the committee treat him like this.'

The outcome was that most of the Stanley Rangers open age team decided to stay at the Travs and renamed themselves Stanley Rangers Old Boys, but then after complaints by the local district committee because the Rangers senior team were being re-formed, they had to change the name again, so they became Stanley Rovers.

Over the next few seasons, Rangers would send spies to our matches, and any minor breach of the rules and we were hauled in front of the Wakefield and District Amatuer Rugby League. But then the inevitable happened, Stanley Rovers made it through to the District Cup final at Belle Vue, home to the Wildcats - our Wembley. And our opponents? Yes it was Stanley Rangers! It must have been one of the best-attended local cup finals in some time, it was also very heated, many players having personal vendettas to settle. As expected, the atmosphere was full of passion and not a little aggression and the game was near boiling point for much of the time. I noticed Dad at the rear of the stand, all alone and I guessed he wasn't happy at the sight of neighbours being at each others throats. Afterwards he told me that although he was glad we won, it saddened him to witness such open animosity.

After the cup final, Alva Palfreyman, chairman of the Rangers, met up with Dad and proposed ending the war. Dad agreed and so they worked out a strategy to win over the members and teams. They spoke with BARLA Chairman, Alan Gibb and Robin Barron of the Sports Council, who both informed them that if the two village teams didn't come together they could never meet the criteria for grant aid from the many differing bodies. So with this information they held a new meeting at the Rangers headquarters and explained that neither team could progress without a merger. The Rangers committee then agreed to merge with Stanley Rovers and the village war ended.

I was made coaching director at Stanley Rangers but recently I've had to relinquish my duties because of coaching commitments at Cas but my cousin Lee, a former professional player with Doncaster and Hunslet, is keeping things progressing. As for Ben Sellers, he had a brief sojourn with the club ensuring the peace became permanent; Alva has now resigned as chairman though he still keeps involved and the present incumbent is Barry Scales, who ironically was against the merger.

12

From Parramatta to the World Cup

The Aussies were coming and Cas had an October date with them. It was the summer training programme prior to the 1994-95 season and boy, was I up for it. I was about to start my ninth season with the club and I was determined to be positive and consistent and on a personal note that is exactly what I achieved, I played thirty games, no subs and scored eleven tries. Gone forever the name super-sub or impact player, I had always wanted to be on from the start in every match, I had always wanted eighty minutes and I had always wanted to play my own game, I had not achieved the latter yet but I would. I had avoided career threatening injuries, I was stronger and fitter than ever but most of all I still had a love for the game and for Castleford.

New goals were in my sights constantly and I held the opinion that with Tawera, Ritchie and Tony, our three international New Zealanders, plus Steady, Tony Smith and Crooksie in the squad, we could hack it with the best.

But the start of the season was frustrating because I had to serve a four match ban courtesy of the disciplinary and Jack Robinson of Wigan who cited me for the Kelvin Skerrett incident. I was given short shrift but I know that had this happened in Australia, I would have had no case to answer because I didn't attack, I merely defended. Anyway, Lee Crooks helped me through the frustration and I came out of it with a much tougher mental approach to my game. I realised I might be too late to make the test team but I was determined to try.

When the Aussies turned up at Wheldon Road, Crooksie, myself and Richard Russell faced Lararus, Walters and Harrogan. I was voted Man of the Match and even though we finished up on the losing side, it was unanimous that we were more than a match for our illustrious opposing front three. However eight different props were to figure for England during the tests but I wasn't one of them, but this only spurred me on because I was certain that if I maintained form, my chance would come. JJ and Lee sang my praises as did the media then another Man of the Match performance at Headingly in the Regal Trophy quarterfinal against Leeds but this time with Ellery Hanley, the Great Britain coach in attendance. We won the match 14-34 and for me it was a double celebration when it was announced that I was picked for the forthcoming European Championships. Ellery had recognised my efforts and I was in the squad at last.

Wigan brought us all down to earth with a bump by comfortably dispatching us in the semi-final of the Regal Trophy, but I put my disappointment behind me as Cas took on Halifax at Thrum Hall. I was maintaining my form, scored the first try and made clean busts to lay on two more. Then disaster struck as Mark Preston, Halifax's winger and former Wigan flyer was put clear. I went into overdrive to cut him off but he suddenly cut inside. He was in full flight and travelling at the speed of light when I swung my left arm instinctively and struck the upper part of his chest including the top of the ball, and Preston went backwards and upwards assisted by my determination to stop him scoring under the posts. The crowd responded as though Mark had been decapitated. I knew he wasn't hurt too bad but he milked it and the referee in his infinite wisdom decided I should take an early bath. My protests fell on deaf ears, the incident was clumsy, yes, malicious, no.

I was a pretty forlorn figure in the ensuing days, a big ban would probably lose me my GB place and undo nine long years of hard graft. Dad agreed to represent me at the disciplinary. 'I'll have a word with young Preston, meanwhile get hold of a wheelchair for me to use at the hearing because it always worked for Perry Mason.'

Well Dad contacted Mark Preston and pleaded. 'Mark if you will speak in Dean's favour, as a family we would be eternally grateful, he didn't do it intentionally he'll assure you and I'm sure no serious damage occurred. What about it Mark, help out a fellow professional realise his lifelong dream to represent his country?'

'I'm sorry Mr Sampson, I can't do that, I had a bruise on my shoulder and it hurt for a few days, no I'm not able to help.'

Dad replaced the receiver. 'Soft bastard, no wonder Wigan sold him.'

At the hearing, Dad didn't bother with the wheelchair and I got another four match ban. I wouldn't have minded so much but two four match bans in less than twelve months didn't exactly make for a glowing record and that hurt.

Something my form and consistency had achieved brought an unexpected bonus, a contract with Parramatta in Australia. So I flew out at the end of the season and arrived at Kingford Smith Airport, Sydney, around nine o'clock on Thursday morning and the rest of the day was spent doing media interviews. In 1990 as a fresh faced rookie at the Gold Coast Seagulls, I was not prepared for the Aussie press and their journalistic licence and I lived to regret one or two of the bold statements that were attributed to me. However, this time I was five years wiser and not about to make the same mistake. I was polite and reserved in my answers and really talked up the Australian game but I decided not to say too much about myself, I would let my performances on the field do my talking.

I was to be billeted with Parramata's other English import ,Vince Fawcett, in a very palatial three bedroom apartment in a block half-a-mile from the stadium. Thursday night I was introduced to my teammates but some seemed none too happy that I was there. The front rowers were less than warm in their reception of me, but no skin off my nose, after all if they were so good then why had I been invited over? I am a big believer that you earn respect and I would win these guy's over on the training paddock and playing field. Then on the Friday, I was invited to go with the squad for a round of 'pub golf' after training. Vince and I met the other guys in the Rose and Crown pub at the end of our street and the rules were explained. Each pub had a par, a par three meant you had to drink three midis (just under half a pint) to par that pub, if you drank four midis then you were one under, if you drank two midis then your score card read one over and so on. We were to visit nine hostelries over the course of the evening and our scorecards would be tallied at the end to find a winner.

Vince and I decided to set the early pace and push the Aussies hard and we left the first pub three under. By the time Vince and I left the sixth pub, we were both over ten under and the game was cancelled as we had left a trail of broken men in our wake. Brett Plowman the big winger signed from Brisbane Broncos was the only exception, now that boy could really drink.

My debut was away at Canberra the following Sunday, the teams drove down on Saturday morning to stay at a motel in Queanbeyan overnight, and let's just say that the myth of Australian professionalism and pre-match preparation was blown apart for me that night. The following day we got walloped 50-12. I came off the bench but unfortunately spent ten minutes in the sin bin for giving Canberra full back Brett Mullins a slap - we would cross swords again. Then I spent ten minutes in the blood bin with a busted nose, welcome to the ARL pommie! But I must have done something right though as I made the starting line up for the next weekends home game against Brisbane Broncos and this game brought about one of the strangest turn of events I've ever witnessed on a rugby field.

Brisbane were up at the top of the table and Parramatta were next to the bottom; a mismatch if you ever saw one on paper but we Parra boys hadn't read the script and found ourselves leading 14-6 a couple minutes from half time when the game took a dramatic twist. The Broncos worked their way up the field before diminutive halfback Allan Langer put up a towering bomb. I'd gone to put pressure on Langer and just at that moment of impact he raised his arm and crack, my hand went numb, pain shot up my arm and I was in agony. To make matters worse, the ball hit the ground and a Broncos attacker was first to it, try to Brisbane. The Parra guys gathered under the sticks - or what was left of the Parra team for as I looked over my shoulder a scene of carnage greeted my eyes. Michael Appleby (the lock) was being escorted from the field by a trainer obviously in great discomfort, his index finger ripped from the socket, Robbie Muchmore, our right centre was helped off with a dislocated shoulder, but worst of all my housemate and fellow Brit Vince Fawcett, was being carried from the field with ruptured knee ligaments. Just ten of us stood behind the sticks waiting for the conversion kick. I looked down at my right hand it had ballooned to twice the size, shit! I was having no luck, one set of six tackles had seen us lose four players with serious injures. Then the halftime hooter sounded, 14-12 to us, an upset was still on the cards.

The dressing room was like a scene from ER, I summoned a trainer and showed him my hand and he immediately called for the doctor. 'What's the verdict doc?' I asked.

'It's definitely broken.'

'No shit Einstein.'

'You'll have to come off, you can't play with that.' Said the doc.

Our coach then came over and informed us that there were no subs left and was it possible for me to go back and sit on the bench just in case.

I started laughing. 'You're kidding aren't you?'

The doc examined my hand and explained that it was shot and couldn't be damaged anymore than it already was so if he gave me a shot of Lignocaine and strapped it tight then I would be OK. The hand was needled and strapped, the game restarted and I took my place on the bench. Then the Broncos scored on their second attack – shit! They were in front, but wait, one of our guys was down in back play. As I watched the trainers tend to the player I was praying it wasn't too bad but no such luck he was coming off. 'Dean are you warmed up, you're going back on?' Shouted the trainer. The injection was beginning to work so at least I wouldn't feel anything.

Feel anything - try embarrassment, helplessness, dejection and a multitude of other emotions. In that second half, Brisbane ran around, over and through our depleted team and amassed 48 unanswered points. I think we touched the ball on three occasions and the game ended 60-14 in the Broncos favour. I'd played practically all the second half with a broken hand and if I thought that was going to get their respect, well they didn't seem to show it, they just thought I was mad, which is probably right but that's another story. Vince and I ended up on Monday night in hospital having our respective operations. Vince's season was over and I was scheduled to be sidelined for eight to ten weeks, however I was back playing in six - pay for play contracts are a great motivation.

While I was recovering, I asked Dad to arrange for my mum and Becky, my sister to come over with my wife Lorraine and our daughter Olivia. Dad went to his bank and asked them for a £5,000 loan while my money came through (I had signed contracts worth over £50,000 to play for Castleford, the new Super League and Paramatta). But the bank turned him down despite being given copies of my contracts and an assurance that the loan could be paid back when my money came through in a couple of months. So Dad told them to get stuffed and went elsewhere for the loan and my family flew over. At the time, I was furious, as both my dad and I had been with that bank for years. I remember thinking it was ironic that in professional sport, you have to watch out for rotten bastards and here I was getting abandoned by my local bank!

Having my family in Australia was a real treat and helped me overcome the disappointment of a broken hand, which was potted up to my elbow, but at least not doing full training I was able to take everyone off on sightseeing trips. We visited the Blue Mountains, explored nearby Sydney and spent time down at the beach. Unfortunately they had to head back to England all too soon.

Back home, Dad negotiated me a new contract with Cas and although Parramatta wanted me to stay with them and offered better terms, the thoughts of Super League's inception and a testimonial lay heavily in Castleford's favour. I packed the family back to England, played another five games after the removal of my pot and scored two tries; a rare thing for props down under. I was sad when I had to return, as the lifestyle in Australia is superb and I had enjoyed my time at Parramatta, despite the broken hand.

Arriving back at Cas I was confident I could carry on where I had left off in the previous campaign. The season was to be a truncated one to allow for the switch to summer rugby in 1996 and once again there had been another change in personnel. Gone were Tawera Nikau, Martin Ketteridge, Richie Blackmore, Tony Kemp, Ian Smales, Tony Morrision and Andy Hay. Several new players came in as replacements; Andrew Schick, Brendan Tuuta, Phil Eden, Adrian Flynn, Tony Marchant - who returned after a stint with Bradford and Lee Harland who joined from Halifax. Apart from Crooksie and Steady, I was now the most senior player, which gave me added responsibility as the season got under way.

I maintained my form and I was included in the England squad for the 1995 World Cup, with Australia at Wembley first up. Karl Harrision and Andy Platt got the nod over me and Paul Broadbent, based on proven experience, but we weren't the only ones to be disappointed as Bobby Goulding had been trying to shift Shaun Edwards for ages. He consoled 'Beans' and myself. 'We can take it out of Fiji on Wednesday.' And that's exactly what happened. We beat Australia 20-16 and then I was named at number ten for the Fiji game, the venue Wigan and the atmosphere was electric. There were 26,263 people packed into that historic stadium and my wife and dad were amongst them - just - they had missed the turn off then stayed on the motorway system and were almost back in Yorkshire via Sheffield when Dad decided to tell Lorraine to turn around. but after a few more detours they made their seats just in time for the national anthem. I told Dad later that it made my hair stand on end, he concurred. 'Same for me son, a long time coming and I was very proud too.'

The Fijians were physical but we won the game convincingly, 46–0. Phil Larder, the coach, praised our performance but my main concern was would I make the next match? I had learned from this experience and I was named at sub against South Africa at Headingly. We won the match, again 46-0 and I scored a try coming off the bench. Then I was again picked for the team against Wales in the semi-final.

Wales proved a stiffer test and put up a brave show but we came out on top 25–10. Unfortunately, I got a broken nose in an accidental clash of heads with Iestyn Harris. I took a real crack because the bleeding wouldn't stop even when plugged, so I had to sit out the rest of the game on the sideline but it didn't stop me celebrating the win with the rest of the team.

Australia were to be our opponents in the final and I prayed I might make the subs spot but alas no such luck, Gary Connelly who had been out ill returned and I was omitted. I had experienced disappointment before but never anything to compare with not making that Wembley final. Australia went on to win the game 16-8 and I had a Centenary World Cup runners-up medal to my name. Reflecting on the World Cup afterwards, I was proud that I had represented my country and pleased that the team had made it to the final, but I couldn't help wondering if I would ever fulfil my dream of facing the Aussies in an international. At the time I felt like the donkey with the carrot, the prize always just in front but never quite able to reach it.

13

Three Fields

One might think when reading the title for this chapter that it indicates my favourite playing areas, well that's not the case, but seeing as I've got on to the subject, Wheldon Road, now the Jungle, has always been number one in my heart and always will be. And while we are following a theme, my second choice is Headingly which although the playing surface of today is a far cry from the late 1980s and 90s it is still a ground with a magical atmosphere - euphoria or heartbreak, depending how we have faired against our old and bitter rivals Leeds or in some other big game. Now my number three probably won't be on too many peoples list but I have my reasons. Both my dad and Uncle Malcolm started their careers at Wakefield Trinity so walking out on Belle Vue's turf always gives me an extra buzz and a proud feeling of following in their footsteps.

But I'm digressing so back to the three fields in the title. We all have childhood memories, some of which remain vivid others obscure, but one such memory I clearly recall was when I was about thirteen years old and living at the Ship pub at Lee Moor. This particular day I arrived back at the pub from playing rugby, I threw my kit bag in the back kitchen and asked mum if I could have a pint of still orange, she duly obliged and I made my way out front. It was a warm sunny day so I sat down onto one of the rustic benches and began to relax watching the world go by.

Lee Moor at that time was as if seemingly in a time warp, then slowly but surely from my left old Mr Scott our retired milkman approached and when he was alongside the table he rapped his cane on the bench. 'Move over young Sammy and let an old man have a rest.'

I eased along the bench and moved my drink. Mr Scott's eyes fixed on the still orange then he produced a hanky and began to mop his brow, simultaneously removing his straw trilby and placing it by my side. 'Gives a man and boy a reason to sleck t'wod cleck young Dean, dunt tha think?'

'Certainly does Mr Scott, would you like a wet of my drink?' I replied

'Certainly not, but be a good lad an go tell thi mother her boyfriend wants a pint of best, off tha goes.'

I ran into the pub and Mum poured him a creamy topped pint. When I re-emereged Mum was passing trivial pleasantries with Mr Scott then I noticed my drink was at a lower level down the glass, I thought you crafty old bugger you must have had a quick swig of my drink while I was in the pub ordering your pint. I sat back down on the bench and Mum returned into the pub, then looking up the hill I espied about ten cyclists freewheeling down toward Mr Scott and myself. Suddenly the lead rider dressed in a very colourful outfit swerved over and pulled up only a couple of feet away from us, the others each in turn drew to a halt, all perspiring heavily, some began to drink from their flasks while others towelled their brows. The lead rider had introduced himself to Mr Scott who had paused before replying and replacing his trilby, the rider said they were from Scarborough Cycling Club and were heading for Chesterfield, unfortunately, they were lost, and could Mr Scott help? Scotty raised himself onto unsteady legs lifted his cane and pointed west. 'All I knaw is it's over thea'. If tha folla's this road to bottom of hill an turns right tha's no but three fields away.'

'Oh thanks very much,' replied the rider, then suddenly as if filled with new vigour, 'follow me chaps, not far now.' And as quickly as they had arrived they were gone. As they passed, the last rider nodded in appreciation to the both of us and Mr Scott looked decidedly pleased with himself, as he slowly sat back on the bench, he took a large swig of beer followed by a belch and wiping his lips with the back of his hand stated. 'What a beautiful day.' Meanwhile I was still trying to fathom out the directions he had given the cyclist's, and eventually my inquisitive nature got the better of me. Now geography wasn't my top subject but I reckoned Mr Scott had got his directions wrong, so I asked him. 'How many fields did you say those cyclists were away from Chesterfield?'

'Three young Dean, three exactly; Wakefield, Huddersfield and Sheffield, I couldn't tell a lie.' He said wryly and with a wink.

Sadly like many other characters Mr Scott passed away last year at a ripe old age but he left me a much wiser boy and at that time, probably left ten cyclist feeling rather confused. I'm sure they would have reached their destination and I like to think they would have had a good laugh if they solved the riddle of three fields from Lee Moor to Chesterfield.

14

A Great Adventure

The commencement of Super League with all the razzmatazz and attention it generated was an exciting time. And although the game itself changed little, there were one or two differences such as dealing with the demands on a weekly basis of warm weather rugby - and the different tape measure used for measuring ten metres by referees Stuart Cummings and Karl Kirkpatrick. Stuart had for many years staggered and stumbled to keep even seven metres, but it suited Stuart's fitness level, whereas Karl was like a kangaroo bouncing about super fit, but I'm sure his ten strides were one and a half metres each resulting in the two teams miles apart and high scoring games. There were other little anomalies that were deemed 'teething problems', including the furore over proposed mergers and none-mergers and I remember at one pre-season game away at Post Office Road, the Featherstone fans started chanting: 'Fev is Fev and Cas is Cas, so stick your merger up your ass!' I guess the authorities didn't take into account the strength of feeling for the local team in some of the Rugby League communities.

Anyway, as for Cas, well, our early season form was like a damp squib, four or five losses consecutively and panic stations all round, I don't profess that I knew then, or do now, exactly where lay the crux of our problems but this season there was something not right from the outset. A few in the squad didn't seem so committed to the cause although most of the team including myself, knuckled down but I had my loyalty to Cas severely tested in the next few months.

In the pre season friendly against Featherstone, we were thoroughly awful and deservedly got beaten - a real wake up call. Then the following week it was Salford at home in the Challenge Cup. Now this was my lowest moment at Cas because of those who had played against Featherstone, I was the only one left out of the whole squad. It was a bitter pill to swallow so I saw my dad prior to the match. 'Get me a move Dad and I mean it - I want away.'

Dad had acted as my agent for most of my career and he knew I was serious, so he contacted John Joyner. 'I'm afraid he's serious John, I feel very uncomfortable about this you being a good friend and Dean being my son. I feel as if I've got a foot in both camps.'

John gave Dad assurances that he knew my abilities and asked him to persuade me to be patient. But this fell on deaf ears, as far as I was concerned I had been at Cas ten years and perhaps it was right to move on. I remember I was unbending to Dad's response so he called John and told him he would have to approach Castleford's Football Director, Jack Fulton. Dad reported back that Jack had promised to bring it up at the next board meeting but when he next spoke to him, Jack was edging. 'Ask the lad to be patient David, we will sort it out.'

But then shocks all round as JJ and Cas parted company after the team had lost five consecutive games; 0-4 away at Salford, 14-22 at home to Wigan, 12-29 away at Halifax, 12-38 at home to Bradford and 20-42 at Sheffield. It was a sad time as for twenty-five long years, John had been a fixture at the club, surely after such service he deserved a place on the board as the football liaison director. I knew John would be bitter and hurt, his emotions mixed and confused, that's how Dad was when it happened to him. When you lose something you love it's gut wrenching, like going through a divorce really, it's far different from just moving clubs. But such is the precarious life of professional sport, one minute you are coach of the year then within a few months you're axed, it can't be right. The knives must have been out for John before my transfer request, I can't flatter myself that it had anything to do with my asking for a move in fact I don't believe Jack Fulton ever brought it before the board, I certainly never got any feedback. I was sorry at the outcome and simply vowed to keep knuckling down and perform where it mattered. Mick Morgan and Lee Crooks stepped into the breach temporarily then after loosing another couple of games, Stuart Raper was announced as John Joyner's replacement.

I didn't know Stuart from Adam but my career under his coaching was about to blossom - coincidence? Probably good fortune mixed with maturity on my part, Stuart's coaching skills, plus a free reign to perform on the pitch made for the right ingredients at the right time. Stuart Raper had started his playing career at Cronulla in the early 1980s. Then after playing for several teams, including Oldham when they beat Wigan in the 1986 Challenge Cup, he started coaching, first with Eden then back at Cronulla, before moving to Cas. At the time the team didn't know much about Stuart other than he'd turned down the chance to coach the Aussie under 19 side to take over from John Joyner, but we soon came to respect him both for his abilities and the way he worked with and motivated the team. Stuart was young and ambitious, a refreshing character and he gave me responsibility for my own performance for the first time in my career. I was entering the arena with the freedom to play my own game. 'Do it your way and if it works then okay and if not we can talk about it.' No more fear of being sidelined at the drop of a hat as I had been before for many years. Early in my playing career under Dad, being sub was explained away that I was young and my time would come. When Darryl came along, even if you played four or five games that were stormers, one drop in form and it was back to the A-team or on the bench. I felt he was inconsistent because he did not apply it to everyone, and while that is a little gripe at Darryl, he did teach or instil many attributes to my game, I just feel his lack of tolerance and flexibility detracted from him becoming a truly great coach.

Darryl was a disciplinarian with a ruthless streak; I remember one time we had to be at a morning training session at nine-thirty. I had agreed to take my sister back to Doncaster as Dad was coaching and living over in Armthorpe, unfortunately even though I had set off at eight o'clock, my car broke down on the motorway going east so I rang my dad. 'I'll be as quick as possible.' He replied, and fifteen minutes later he passed us going west to the next junction. Ten minutes later he picked me and Becky up but we had to go east until the next junction then back towards Cas. Dad sensed I was nervous as time was ticking by, I explained it was a £50 fine if you were late and so Dad put his foot down to the boards. He pulled up into the ground less than a minute late, I had my boots on and was in the dressing room even before some of the other players but in my heart, I knew I would be fined; such was Darryl's authoritarian attitude. When I told Dad afterwards he was flabbergasted. 'A player should be commended for going to such lengths.' He remarked. And there lies the difference between two experienced coaches, but as players we must adapt accordingly.

I vividly recall Stuart's first game in charge against St Helens at Anfield, home of Liverpool Football Club. We performed creditably but suffered the inevitable defeat, just as we did in the next game, but

Stuart was slowly turning things around. Then came our first victory 12-10 at home to Salford, followed by picking up points in six of the last eleven games that season, including a memorable 35-16 home win against St Helens. At the end of the season, the players and Stuart were the toast of the town, you would have thought we had won the league never mind just survived it, such was the fear of relegation at that time and the suspicions of mergers and uncertainty of what the future held.

15

The Testimonial

As everyone knows, a testimonial is the recognition and reward for the years of loyal service a player has given to one club. I believe the criteria used by the rugby league are normally ten years and 250 matches. So these days it's becoming a rarer and rarer occurrence due to freedom of contracts and regular movements by players from club to club. Anyhow, the financial rewards are also tempered by the now much improved contracts that rugby league players receive in the game today thanks to Uncle Rupert and his News Corporation outfit.

Well, the Dean Sampson testimonial came about in 1997 after 12 seasons and over 300 games with Castleford. Now I have seen many and supported most testimonials, so I was well aware of the hard work that it would entail and also of the great financial remuneration that it could bring to the loyal individual. The original concept was to reward loyal players when wages in the game were in keeping with the working mans. Yes, I got a new improved contract and I was earning good money, but nothing like what I would have received had I chased the pot of gold that the Australian rugby league had dangled in front of me. But I should have seen the writing on the wall early on, as I found it almost impossible to assemble a benefit committee. Everyone I spoke to said they would help but no one wanted to commit themselves long-term.

The first job was to arrange my testimonial game, I was in negotiations with Bradford Bulls to bring them down to Castleford pre-season. I was thinking big, the Bulls were the best-supported side in Super League, they would have ensured a bumper crowd and a healthy start to my testimonial year. But not to be, Castleford informed me that they had arranged their pre-season games and we would be playing Hull at the Boulevard and Sheffield at home midweek. My protests fell on deaf ears and as I couldn't really have my testimonial game at the Boulevard, I had only one option left open to me. Now with all due respect to Sheffield, they did not have one of the largest followings of supporters, so combined with a midweek evening kick-off, I could see my testimonial falling flat before it had begun.

Fearing the worst, I approached the board and asked them that seeing as I had had the Bulls lined up, could they give me a guaranteed income from the Sheffield game? Well the board, after much discussion, offered me a guarantee of £15,000 in gate receipts to go to my fund, not what I would have got had we played the Bulls, but I wasn't a greedy man so I agreed. The night of the game came and when I led the team out I was totally gob smacked, the crowd was heaving, what had I ever been worried about? It was a hard fought and close game, as Castelford - Sheffield matches usually were, and at the end, the Eagles just pipped us. Then the crowd was given out, over four thousand five hundred were in attendance that night and with my reckoning (maths being not my strongest subject), a conservative estimate put the takings at around £30,000 and the club had the bar takings to compensate – excellent!

But not-to-be; after the game I showered, had a bite to eat then went to collect my money.

'There you go Dean £15,000 as agreed.' Said the secretary.

'£15,000? Surely we took more than that with over 4,000 in the ground?' I replied.

'Yes but your share was fifteen as agreed.'

'Yes but...'

'Look any problems Dean you will have to sort out with the chief exec tomorrow.'

To cut a long story short, I didn't get anymore money but I suppose the club did honour their guarantee, their argument being that if only a small crowd turned up then they would have been out of pocket. Well not if they'd taken on the Bulls as I planned, anyway I suppose I should be thankful for what I got. But I do think the best gesture to a loyal player would have been for the club to take out its expenses and donate the rest back to the testimonial, instead they had a nice pay-day at my expense.

Later in my testimonial year, things went from bad to worse. An event at Methley Working Men's Club saw about a dozen people turn up, then an organised golf day lost a bucketful of money. We did have some success when we organised a sportsman's dinner at Samsons, our own venue. This event was well supported by my fellow players and we actually showed a profit, but this proved to be only temporary respite from disillusionment as the next event, a big concert at the Cas Civic Centre proved to be a total wash out. We had booked some of the best acts in club land, it had been well advertised via radio, press and posters but I can't express in enough words my disappointment that night when the audience totalled less than artists. I was gutted because we didn't have an answer as to why - was it general apathy to live entertainment or the syndrome 'he's got plenty from Super League anyway', who knows, the entertainment at that Civic Centre show was first class, and any perception that I had plenty of dough was way off the mark. Maybe it's just that the testimonial has had its day.

In the end, what I had made from the Sheffield game slowly dwindled to cover all the losses from the other functions and probably the only testimonial in history to make a loss was mine. Yet I bear no ill feeling, my testimonial coincided with a lull in the clubs fortunes and this probably contributed to its failure.

As Granddad used to say, 'if it doesn't kill you it will only make you stronger'.

16

A Third Trip to Aus

The 1997 season had been a real struggle and as explained before, it is fortunate that we managed to regain some form to escape being relegated. In fact, in the latter part of the season we started to treat each game like a cup final, we threw everything at the opposition in those last couple of months. But the turning point for me and I think the whole team, was the two weeks we spent in Australia together playing in the World Club Challenge against Hunter Mariners and Perth Reds. We lost both games but the opportunity to blow off some steam, the team building and the bonding that took place in those two weeks, I believe saved Castleford from drifting into obscurity. The way Stuart Raper handled the players showed the squad what a good man manager he was, something I'd not thought too highly of in other Australians I had been coached by. However, Stuart knew how to control the players on and off the field, just how much slack to let them have and when to rein them in and everyone responded in the most positive way.

One of Stuart's secrets, I can tell you now as he's no longer my boss, was to get the players who'd just arrived in the hotel after a thirty hour journey from England, on the bus to training within one hour of putting down our cases. I put mine down and fell onto my bed, my roommate was Brendan 'baby faced assassin' Tuuta, and he hit his bed too, only meaning to rest for a couple of minutes. I awoke one hour later with Brendan fast asleep across from me. I looked at my watch. 'Oh fuck Toot's we're late.'

We'd only been in the country a couple of hours and we were already in trouble.

'We'll get fined.' I shouted as I emptied my suitcase out onto the floor; socks, T-shirt, shorts. 'Right, ring reception they might not have set off yet.' But too late, they were gone, Stuart obviously wasn't messing about and had set the example early on, only problem was, me and Toot's were the example again! Then I had a thought, phone a taxi, we might even beat them to the ground. We were jumping into the taxi by ten past and we told the driver. 'An extra ten bucks if you get us to...' Fuck, we didn't know where we were going training, I screamed back at reception. 'Anybody know where Cas tigers are training?'

'Cronulla I think.' The receptionist replied.

The taxi driver did us proud; he got us there in record time. 'Thirty bucks mate, oh plus the extra ten you promised, that makes forty.'

I was in the front and turned around to Toot's for some cash but he was gone – bastard! I paid the driver then raced into the ground and onto the field. Stuarts face looked like thunder, we both apologised profusely and I felt like a frigging kid but with the pressure at home in Super League I didn't want him to think we were treating this trip as a holiday. I hate being late so to do it early on seemed so unprofessional, added to which I was a senior pro and should have been setting the example. Toot's and I jogged onto the field just in time to see our Australian centre, David Chapman, limping off with a torn calf muscle; his tournament was over twenty minutes into the first training session. Half an hour later we were back on the bus,

Toot's and me were the butt of all the jokes. Then Stuart informed us when we got back to the hotel that we had one hour before we met in the bar. Toot's and me were the first to the bar - as if you couldn't have guessed, or so we thought until we saw Stuart was already waiting for us with beer in hand. 'Fancy a beer lads?' We didn't need to be asked twice.

When everyone was in the bar Stuart informed me and Toot's that we were each fined fifty bucks for being late to training. I was ninety dollars down already before my first beer as I still hadn't been paid by Toot's for the taxi, this is going to be one expensive trip I thought. The night went without further incident and everyone began to relax and unwind after a few amber nectars. Training was first thing in the morning in the gym and pool complex on the hotel rooftop so I had an early night leaving several of the boys down in the bar. It was not like me, I can tell you, but I wasn't going to be late twice, so into bed I fell and slept like a baby. The morning came and I felt remarkably clear-headed and fresh, I thought it must be due to the weak Aussie gnats piss they call beer. The morning session was short, sharp but intense and after I'd finished I went and sat in the outside rooftop Jacuzzi with the hot water soothing my aching muscles. As I leaned back and looked out over the Pacific Ocean, the sun high in the sky with not a cloud in sight, I remember thinking to myself, what a job; it doesn't get much better than this, a real Shangri-La. To any aspiring young player who wants to make the grade, I wish I could share that moment with you because when the going gets really tough and the training seems backbreaking, I just think back to moments like those and how lucky I am that rugby league gave me the opportunity to do things I'd only ever dreamed of.

That afternoon, Stuart took us on a trip across town to Shane

Flanagan's local. Shane had been our conditioner the previous season and was a sound bloke, a real character who got on with everyone, again the cold beer flowed freely all afternoon, I was in full flow, my jokes and conversation had everyone in stitches laughing. But I should have smelt a rat; the boys were practically wetting themselves at my every word. An hour or so later I visited the toilet, after washing my hands I looked in the mirror, shock, horror, the bastards! Stuck to my shoulders were at least half a dozen condoms, all-afternoon I'd been talking to the locals and all along I'd had these fucking jonnies hung from me like latex tassels. I pulled them off and exited the gents then as I appeared back in the pub the whole room cracked out laughing, every man, dog and Aussie were pissing themselves at my expense. I tried to laugh it off but inside I was seething. They had got me good and I wasn't a happy chappie.

After the pub, Mike Ford was driving back to the hotel in the mini bus that had been provided at our disposal. Mike was designated the driver as he drank very little - not because he was the consummate pro, which he was anyway - but because two pints and he was pissed as a newt. On the way back, some of the younger players were very drunk and having a great laugh about the condom caper. Two in particular were drinking bottles of beer and when they finished they threw them out of the window onto the road, smashing glass in all directions. I remonstrated with them and things became very edgy. However, the straw that broke the camels back was when we stopped at a set of traffic lights. A guy dressed as a clown was collecting for charity with a big bucket, the boys beckoned him over seemingly fumbling for change. One of the guys held out his hand and as the clown lifted the bucket, he grabbed hold of the handle, words were exchanged and after tugging at the bucket he pulled it from the

A very young Diesel with an angelic face that only a mother could love.

A family portrait, Mum and Dad pose with Becky, Jonathan and me in the early 1980s.

In the beginning. Castleford Under 17s line up at Belle Vue, Wakefield in 1984. I'm in the back row on the left.

In action for Cas during John Tennant's testimonial match at McLaren Field, Bramley.

Picture, Sig Kasatkin

Fartown 1983. Yorkshire Schoolboys take on France.

The Castleford Queen and John Kendrew present me with the Alliance Player of the Year award in my first year as a pro.

My first Yorkshire Cup final at Headingley. The pre-match nerves are there for all to see.

Picture, Sig Kasatkin

On the charge at the Boulevard as I break through tackles by Tim Wilby and Andy Dannats.

Picture, Sig Kasatkin

In the company of greats, Kev Beardmore and Kev Ward, both inspirational in my early years.

Picture, Sig Kasatkin

Elland Road and dreams come true as we hammer Bradford in the Yorkshire Cup final.

Picture, Sig Kasatkin

On the Wembley pitch before the 1992 Challenge Cup final looking resplendent in my club blazer.

Picture, Sig Kasatkin

The 1992 Challenge Cup final. I offer my political opinions to the then Prime Minister, John Major.

Relaxing with Steve Hampson, Gary Schofield and Lee Crooks on the journey home after the 1992 Lions tour.

June 5th 1993, Lorraine makes me the happiest man in the world.

The notorious 1994 Premiership final at Old Trafford.

Picture, Sig Kasatkin

Enjoying a well deserved break (quite literally) post Premiership 1994.

*Cas lads celebrate. Tony 'Casper' Smith and myself enjoy the
moment after beating Fiji at Central Park in the 1995 World Cup.*

Picture, Sig Kasatkin

*I feel the full force of Wales back
rower Paul Moriarty in the 1995
World Cup semi-final at Old
Trafford.* Picture, Sig Kasatkin

*With my wife Lorraine enjoying
the Australian sunshine in the
magnificent Blue Mountains.*

Lawrence of Castleford takes in the pyramids.

My one and only GB test cap against Australia at Wembley in 1997. Picture, Sig Kasatkin

The 1997 end of season presentation and a clean sweep for yours truly.

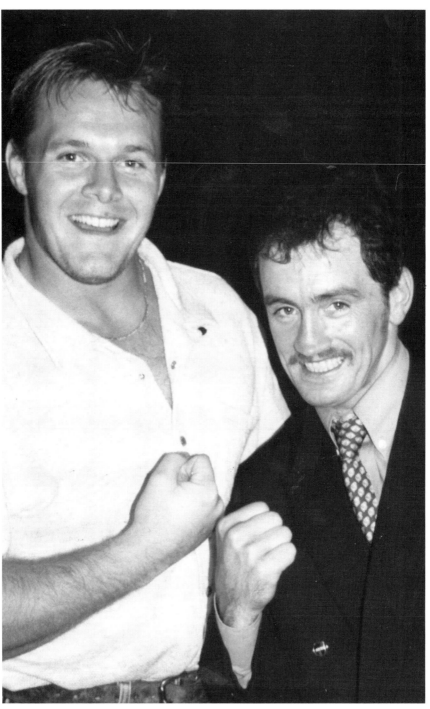

I get to meet a true champion. Me and Barry McGuigan at Dads pub, Samson's in Stanley.

The next generation. My beautiful kids Olivia and Joe.

Showing my son Joe the tricks of the trade.

Like father like daughter: Olivia (back row second from left) gets ready to make her Jungle debut with Stanley Rangers Under 8s.

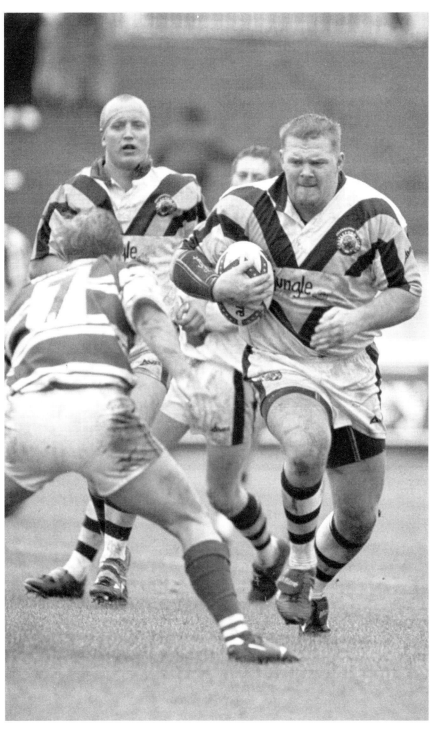

On the charge, as Halifax close in. Picture, Sig Kasatkin

Taking the ball up against our old enemy the Rhinos supported by my good mate Aaron Raper.   Picture, Sig Kasatkin

Aunt Connie, Uncle Brian and I support Dad at the launch of his book.

Leading out the Tigers on my 400th appearance. A moment that will live with me forever.

Picture, Sig Kasatkin

After years of struggle I finally made the number ten shirt my own.

Picture, Sig Kasatkin

clowns grasp. Then the lights turned green and Fordy, oblivious to what was going on behind him, began to move off. As he accelerated, the clown went from a walk to a jog to a flat out sprint holding onto his bucket; Linford Christie couldn't have done better. Looking back now, I can see the funny side of it but at the time, the sight of a screaming clown sprinting beside a bus his bucket stuck fast to the window was not top of my comedy memories. I bawled at the player to let go, eventually he relented and the clown, his bucket and a heap of loose change went flying through the air. Well that was it, I lost the plot, I was seeing red. The two players told me to shut up and stop being a tosser so I challenged them there and then. 'Come on then, right now, both of you.' The drink, the condom prank, the smashed bottles, the clown, all of it just exploded. Now whatever happens, team mates should always stick together, but I crossed the line and while I regretted it afterwards, it was too late. They knew I meant it and I don't think they fancied taking me on so the rest of the journey was completed in silence. I guess in retrospect I'd made my point.

After a tough training session on the Wednesday, Stuart informed us that all the players would be visiting his local down at Cronulla, where we would be having a bit of a reception and Stu's family would be joining us. When we arrived, I was introduced to Stuart's father the legendary Johnny Raper who regaled us with tales of his past exploits which captivated us all evening. I later read Johnny's book 'The Man in the Bowler Hat' and realised the significance of Johnny's influence on Stuart.

The end of the night came and Johnny made a couple of phone calls - that man knew everybody. 'Boys, if you go into town to the Cross (an area of Sydney renowned for it's night life) call in on my mate at his bar and he will look after you.'

So into town we went and true to Johnny's word, the guy did us proud. Come the early hours of the morning, I was ready for bed but my drinking buddies, Rich 'the fish' McKell and Jason 'hollow legs' Lidden, moved our party onto the famous Sydney watering hole the Bourbon and Beefsteak. That night I saw plenty of bourbon but bugger all of the beefsteak, then at seven o'clock in the morning, the three of us staggered from the bar, into a taxi and back to the hotel.

Now drinking for ten hours solid might sound bad enough to normal folk but we had to be at training by nine, just two hours away, no chance of going to bed, just a cold shower, half a dozen cups of coffee and a gallon of water. Then to make matters worse Stuart informed us on our arrival at Cronulla to do a gym session, there would be TV cameras to do a pre-match story on the Sunday game at Newcastle, and they wanted to get a few interviews. I began to panic I was in no fit state to talk to myself never mind an Aussie reporter so sensing my obvious reluctance to play ball Stuart, remarkably calm given the circumstances, whispered to me. 'Keep a low profile; maybe even disappear until the cameras have gone.'

So I retreated to the relative safety of the toilet block, picked a cubicle, and sat myself on top of the cistern with my legs wedged fast against the door. I closed my eyes and that was that. It only seemed like minutes, but I was told I'd been gone an hour and a half. I was rudely awakened by Graham Steadman banging on the door and shouting my name, apparently the cameras had gone and the weights session had finished thirty minutes earlier. I was nowhere to be found, so the players, coaches and staff turned the Cronulla stadium upside down until I was spotted through the tiny toilet window, I was not the most popular person on the bus ride back to the hotel as everyone just wanted to hit the sack and sleep and I had held everything up. Some of the players were so pissed off they'd taken a taxi back to the hotel and didn't even bother to join in the search.

That Thursday afternoon we departed for Newcastle to face the Hunter Mariners on the Sunday, and by the time the match came around, there were no more cliques, no us and them, we were one solid unit and to top it off not one of us cared if we never saw, never mind tasted alcohol again. Stuart later admitted to me that he had planned it that way all along, it certainly worked as in those two weeks we became a team.

17

Diesel's Castleford Dream Team

When my dad wrote his book, he compiled a dream team comprising players he had played either with or against. Such was the length of his career, he included many who were at their peak long before I was born but also a few that I played with when I turned professional. Anyway, this is the part of the book where my personal preferences come to the fore and given I've been fortunate to play through my entire professional career with Cas, and the wealth of talented players I've turned out with over that time, I have decided to list my dream team made up only of my Wheldon Road colleagues.

Now no doubt many of the readers won't agree with my selection. Cas fans will probably have their own favourites which I've not included and fans of other teams will probably think I'm guilty of nepotism for not including anyone from other clubs. But I stand by my selection and I'm sure that each player at his peak would have made up a team that could stand the test, not just at domestic level but in international matches too. Anyway, everyone is entitled to their opinion and if you see me sometime then maybe we'll have a pint and debate the matter.

For the record my dream team is:

1. Graham Steadman

I've chosen Graham not because he's the Cas coach, but because his electrifying pace and ability to step off either foot made Steady one of the greatest attacking full backs of all time. Cas spent a record £176,000 to bring Steady from our neighbours Featherstone Rovers and it was money well spent.

2. St John Ellis

Singe joined Cas from York and quickly established himself as a very exciting winger who knew where the try line was. Never lacking in self-confidence, Singe had his best years playing outside Kiwi Richie Blackmore, but could also slip back to full back without losing any of his attacking potency. A real character who entertained just as much with his wise cracks in the dressing room as on the field with his stylish play.

3. Richie Blackmore

Ritchie was dogged by shoulder injures when he joined the club but after surgery he showed the natural ability that had taken him into the Kiwi test side. A powerful runner with amazing hands, he could create chances out of nothing, just ask Singe. Ritchie was also another character who the fans adored.

4. Tony Marchant

With both Tony and me working together with the academy squad, we are always retelling the tales of a past era, but it serves to remind me of Tony's qualities as a player, a supremely fit athlete with great pace who I don't think I ever saw him miss a tackle. His try at Wembley in the 1986 Challenge Cup victory over Hull KR will long stand in my memory and his partnership with his winger Dave 'Denzil' Plange usually left opponents coming off second best in all departments.

5. David Plange

A raw talent that came from that hot bed of rugby league; Scunthorpe! Denzil was a block-busting, powerful winger who loved to inflict maximum damage to the opposition. His no nonsense aggressive style perfectly complemented Tony Marchant's which is why I have picked the pair of them for my team.

6. John Joyner

A club record with over 600 appearances, three Lions tours, twenty years as a Castleford player, JJ had it all. A great competitor with wonderful skills, it was a joy and an honour just to appear alongside John, he was probably the most naturally gifted player I ever appeared with. I had my differences with John when he was the Castleford coach but I still have the utmost respect for him. No doubt many will say John was a centre but when I played alongside him he was at either six or thirteen.

7. Danny Orr

Even at a young age it was obvious that Danny had tremendous potential. Then starting as a hooker with the first team steeled his defensive qualities before his transition to the halfback position, which saw Danny leap to superstar status. Becoming the clubs youngest captain and with his pace and deception troubling even the tightest of defences, it's a travesty Danny hasn't won more international recognition.

8. Lee Crooks

Lee's reputation was much maligned when he was at Leeds but his arrival at Cas, again for a world record fee, saw a rebirth for this most gifted of front rowers. I played in many memorable games with Lee and he was an inspiration to me. The hard work he put in to developing his skills, keeping himself fit and often playing with injuries had to be seen to be believed. As tough as teak but a nicer person you couldn't wish to meet.

9. Aaron Raper

Aaron just pushes out Kev Beardmore for my team, he was a fantastically talented player, a tough defender, who had class stamped all over him. A real competitor with more tricks than a magician, I learnt so much from playing alongside Aaron. His time at the club coincided with some of my best rugby and I can only thank him for that. If he had been as fast as he was funny, he'd probably have been one of the all time greats.

10. Kevin Ward

Growing up in Stanley and watching Kevin Ward in his early days was something special. He was a role model and everyone's hero, a supremely powerful, hard-as-nails front rower revered by the Aussies and worshipped by Cas and Saint's fans alike. I tried to emulate Kevin's style but there is and always will be only one Kevin Ward.

11. Keith England

I don't recall 'Beefy' ever taking a backward step in a game. He was a destructive defender who loved doing the tough stuff; he had no time for reputations and often destroyed them. Not the most naturally gifted of players but he certainly made up for it with his enthusiasm and phenomenal work rate. One of the first names on my team sheet.

12. Ron Gibbs

To fully appreciate 'Rambo's' defensive destructiveness you had to play alongside him. He would often come whistling by your ear, his body parallel to the floor, impacting with the opposing player in mid-flight. A truly terrifying tackler but Ronnie was also a very skilful player who could attack with the best of them. I also played alongside him in Australia for Gold Coast - I wasn't going anywhere unless he was in the team! Ronnie always gave value for money and who can forget the old scrum down programme when he knocked himself out at Wakefield but refused to leave the field - and nobody was going to dare make him.

13. Adrian Vowles

When John Joyner brought Vowlesy in to play stand-off, the jury was out at Castleford, but his transition to loose forward had immediate results. Passionate and committed are words that don't do justice to this true Man of Steel. When some players would have trouble getting out of bed with injuries, Vowlesy just took them onto the field. Pound for pound, one of the best players I have played alongside and just like the rest of the back row, one of the hardest hitters in defence.

For my subs bench, I've picked team mates who could so easily have made the starting line up, it really is very close but I guess you've got to draw the line somewhere. So here goes:

14. Tony Smith

'Casper', a local lad, who became one of our best halfbacks. A larger than life character who only knew one way to play - at one hundred miles an hour! As quick as they come, Casper worked hard to take all the best attributes of the great players he played alongside and mould them into his own game, it was a sad day when he left to join Wigan.

15. Kevin Beardmore

One of the last of the old school, an international who gave Castleford eleven great years. 'Gripper' was a great hooker whose link with twin Bob bordered on the telepathic. Extremely fit, Kev also had great vision and put me over for numerous tries from dummy half. Great company to be with, a genuinely funny man who always kept the youngsters in check.

16. Tawera Nikau

'T' was the complete back rower, a natural athlete and born leader who was an inspiration both on and off the field. A top performer on both sides of the world who I felt should have had more international caps, T was instrumental in reviving Castleford in the early nineties.

17. Michael Smith

A true game breaker, 'Miffy' is powerful with plenty of pace for a big man. He has all the talent in the world and when he realises this, he will go on to greater things. Hopefully he'll be wearing a Castleford shirt for many years to come.

Drawing up my dream team has been the hardest part of writing this book. Having played for so long with Cas and alongside so many great players - far too many to mention - it was nearly impossible to decide my final seventeen. But the guys I have picked have not only been great players, they have also had an impact on my career and performances. The halfbacks were especially hard to decide with so much quality to chose from Including Bob Beardmore, Gary French, Brad Davis, Mike Ford, Tony Kemp and Mitch Healey to name but a few. The coach of this team would have to be Stuart Raper as Steady and JJ are already playing. Stuart's affect on my game is greatly appreciated he respected me as a player and gave me responsibility and influence. I think I probably played my best rugby under Stuart's guidance and feel that if he coached this side then Castleford certainly would have had the glory they so richly deserve. And before you ask - no I don't think I would have got in.

1. Graham Steadman

2. St John Ellis   5. David Plange

3. Richie Blackmore   4. Tony Marchant

6. John Joyner

7. Danny Orr

13. Adrian Vowles

11. Keith England   12. Ronnie Gibbs

8. Lee Crooks   9. Aaron Raper   10. Kevin Ward

Subs: 14. Tony Smith   Coach: Stuart Raper

15. Kevin Beardmore

16. Tawera Nikau

17. Michael Smith

18

A Matter of Honour

The phone call came through to the Rangers clubhouse about six o'clock on Saturday evening. 'Dean can you ring home it's urgent.' I had been watching my team, Stanley Rangers, that afternoon then gone to the clubhouse for a few beers with the boys after the game. On phoning home, I was told that Phil Lowe, the Great Britain manager, was trying to reach me. I had been part of the squad for three weeks but had been released from the camp as Andy Goodway would not be requiring my services for the last game against Australia at Elland Road. Working my way back from a dislocated ankle in seven weeks to play in the first test at Wembley was I thought not bad going, the time and effort I put into rehab and maintaining my fitness didn't bear thinking about. I had played twenty minutes against the Aussies at Wembley off the bench and I was the proudest man in the country, my first, and sadly, my last test cap. The following week GB coach Andy Goodway had pulled me to one side during training at the South Leeds Stadium and informed me that as he was worried about my general fitness I wouldn't be figuring in the last two tests. I was gutted, all that hard work and sacrifice, but at least I'd had those twenty minutes at Wembley against Australia. Andy went on to tell me that when I was fit and my form was good I'd be the first front rower on his team sheet, so I thought get myself in shape for next seasons internationals then.

When I contacted Phil Lowe at the Village Hotel in Leeds, he informed me that Paul Broadbent was doubtful for the third test as he had picked up a training injury the previous day and could I come in as cover as a decision on his fitness would be made in the morning.

Christ I'd just sunk about six pints after the Rangers game, not the best preparation for a test match. I asked Phil to give me a couple of hours and I would be there, I just had one or two things to sort out, for instance a shower, brush my teeth about twenty times and eat half-a-dozen packets of mints. In the end, I need not have bothered as Paul passed his fitness test and took his place in the starting line up. Phil asked me to stay on as there were several jobs that needed doing and would I help muck in. Well, I thought, not a problem at least I would get to see the game for free.

Phil designated me with the vitally important role of sand boy. Now you may laugh but when you are sand boy to goal kicker Andy Farrell, the slightest error in sand consistency is met with a volley of abuse. My first venture onto the field for one of Andy's kicks was met by: 'It's too fucking dry, sort it out.' On my second attempt it was dismissed as: 'It's now too fucking wet, get it sorted.' The pressure may have been on Andy but that was no reason to take it out on me, I was there voluntarily anyway. So on my third visit to the field I was taking no chances, I jogged over with the bucket of sand in one hand and a bottle of water in the other, on reaching Andy I dropped them on the floor and said, 'there, now you can mix it yourself.' If looks could kill, I'd now be six feet under. We got stuffed, yes, and I might have only been the sand boy but I played my part.

The post match banquet was held in a posh Leeds hotel, great, I'll have some of that I thought so I phoned my wife Lorraine, told her to get her best dress on and meet me there. Lorraine looked a million dollars when she arrived and we proudly took our seats alongside Brian McDermott and his wife. I'd roomed with Brian for the first test down in London. The Friday afternoon I saw Brian receive a phone call from his brother Paul, he then asked if he could have some time alone. The next day Brian had a massive game against the Aussies and only when we were back in Wakefield, walking up Westgate, did he disclose what had happened. Brian apologised for his sombre mood that weekend but the phone call he had received on the Friday from his brother was to inform him of his father's death. Here was Brian apologising and he'd just lost his father, turned out in the test match and told no one. The way Brian coped was a lesson to me, it spoke volumes of his bravery, and he handled the situation better than I ever could have.

At the Leeds post match banquet, the free booze flowed and everyone had their fare share; jugs of lager and bitter, carafes of wine, even the odd short, it was all available and consumed with relish - or was that just me? After the meal had ended and the speeches given, the party began to break up, some people going home, some into town, others like myself and Lorraine had a leisurely walk to the Holiday Inn on Wellington Street to meet up with my Castleford coach Stuart Raper for a few beers. This was also the hotel in which the Australian test team were staying, Stuart was catching up with his long time mentor at Cronulla and now Australian coach John Lang. Andy Farrell was there too but I didn't think I was his favourite person, because of the sand saga earlier. Things were going fine, Lorraine was sat across the room with a friend of hers, Claire, who was on a course and staying at the hotel that week. I excused myself and headed for the bathroom but on my return five minutes later the atmosphere in that room seemed very tense and everyone was looking at me. I looked across to where Lorraine was sat and saw she had her head in her hands and seemed to be crying, her friend had her arm around her and knelt in front of Lorraine were two Aussie players, Wendell Sailor and Gordon Tallis. I made my way over to them and asked what the hell was going on. 'There's been an incident but things are OK now.' Wendall replied.

I turned to Wendall and said, 'I wasn't asking you, I was asking my wife, now if you don't mind.'

'It's OK, he's gone now they took him away somewhere.' Lorraine replied.

'Taken who away? What the hell has happened?' Now I was getting mad.

'The one who spat at Lorraine, they took him away.' Added Claire.

'Who spat at you? Why? Where is he?' I shouted.

'Dean just take me home, I want to go home, I want to go now.' Cried Lorraine.

'Not until I've sorted this out.'

Everyone was apologising for what had happened, John Lang, Wendell all of them, but I was still no wiser as to what had actually gone down.

'I'm going home are you coming?' Lorraine said. She had regained her composure and was heading for the door.

'I'm going nowhere until I find out what the hell is going on here.' I said following Lorraine down the steps and out of the front door. I caught hold of her arm and asked her just what had happened, I was shaking with rage. Lorraine spun round, her eyes all puffy and red, full of tears. 'Let's just leave it and go home, I want to go home.'

'No, just tell me what happened and then we'll go home.'

There was a brief moment when Lorraine looked straight at me; she knew I was going nowhere but back into the hotel. 'One of the Aussie players, I don't know who he was came and sat with Claire, he then put his hand on my leg and was coming on to me,' began Lorraine. 'I told him to go away and moved his hand, he pushed his hand back on to my leg and swore at me, so I threw my drink over him and stood up, it was then that he spat on me.'

'He did what to you?' I bellowed.

Lorraine carried on, 'I went to hit him but he spat at me again, if it hadn't been for Claire and those two players then I'm sure he would have hit me, now let's go home please.'

'No, who was he, what did he look like?'

'I don't know, he was tall and skinny, that's all I remember.'

I handed Lorraine a fistful of money and told her to go straight home, I would go and sort this out, she was not happy at me staying but she knew I wasn't going anywhere until I'd dealt with the matter, so she jumped into a taxi and left. As I was walking back into the hotel I was thinking the bastard, no one spits at my wife, who does he think he is? I returned to the bar and began asking questions to find out who was responsible, everyone suddenly seemed to know very little and for a room full of people it was mighty strange that no one had witnessed the incident, whatever the reason no one was willing to give up a name. I decided to be patient and sober up a little, just to be on the safe side, I needed to be sharp and clear headed. The night wore on and people began drifting off to bed, then bingo, they say everything comes to those who wait, the guilty party swaggered back into the room unknown to me until someone let it slip. 'I can't believe he's come back after what he did.' It was just loud enough for me to overhear. I looked over to the door, several of the Aussie players noticed that he had returned to the bar, and they began to usher him back out of the door and, I bet, back to the safety of his room. This was proof enough of his guilt for me, now for the retribution so I sat back, took a sip of my drink and waited. Thirty minutes later when the bar was practically empty, I started making my way down to reception. I asked the night porter if he had an envelope as I had something to return to one of the Aussie players and wanted to put it under his door along with a note to make sure he got back what I owed him. The porter handed me an envelope and asked which player it was, I gave him the name and he replied, 'let me see for you sir, ah yes he's in room 216.'

I walked towards the stairs and began my ascent to the second floor. Walking along the corridor, deserted at this time as it was the early hours of the morning, I came across room 216. What luck, the door opposite was ajar, opening it fully I looked in the room, a player lay comatose on his bed, I walked to the back of the room turned and ran back across, in to the corridor, hitting the door to room 216 with my right shoulder. There was a sound of splintering wood as the door and the casing, collapsed into the room. Quick as a flash, I stepped into the semi-darkness, the offending player shot from his bed, eyes like saucers, seeing me stood before him his jaw dropped. He cried out. 'Wait, no, no, hold on.' But my self control had gone. I rained blow after blow on him until he flopped onto the bed face down and unconscious. Then in sheer frustration at him, I smashed my fist into his back. I thought to myself that will hurt when he sits down on the plane tomorrow, I hoped a reminder on the long journey home of the disgusting way he had behaved toward my wife.

I had taken retribution but I had gained little satisfaction and I was still in a thunderous mood as I turned away from the prone torso only to find Wendell Sailor stood in the doorway. To say he looked shocked was an understatement, an unconscious team-mate, a smashed door and the room in disarray was probably not what he expected, especially if it was his room. 'I'm done with him.' I growled. He stepped aside, I had no argument with Wendell or anyone else in the hotel, but as I left the room and turned to face the walk back along the corridor, the sight that greeted me was, with hindsight, of comical proportions. This long corridor was full of Aussie players all in differing states of undress and all with their eyes transfixed on me. Talk about walking the gauntlet but I'd made my bed and I had to lie in it. I walked through the throng of Aussies who, collectively, could have given me the mother of a hiding, a couple postured another shouted but no one stepped forward. When I approached reception, my pulse rate was noticeably slowing and I apologised to the night porter, handed him my credit card and told him what had happened and that I would return in the morning at ten o'clock.

As I walked out into the early morning air, a feeling of relief passed through me. It is common knowledge that some Aussies often deride the Brits within rugby league, but I knew of one who would keep his mouth shut in future. Apparently, it is alleged that his behaviour when drunk had left a lot to be desired on previous occasions, well then he should cut down or stop because none of his teammates defended him or sought retribution for reasons known only to themselves.

I don't think he ever represented Australia again and that was also to be my last confrontation with the old enemy. Maybe there was some kind of pact between the management, keep the protagonists away, bury the matter, then handshakes all round, whatever, but I would have dearly loved to have faced them on the pitch again.

As for the player who accosted my wife, I'm not going to name him – he's not worth it.

19

A Tiger Walking Tall

I suppose that with the relegation dogfight behind us it was inevitable that everyone involved was determined never to tread that path again. Danny Orr emerged to prominence, plus with Adrian Vowles, Francis Maloney, Richie McKell and Michael Smith who signed along with Gael Tallec and Danny Ellison from Wigan and for the first time we had a twenty-five man squad. The summer had given Stuart the chance to work on a consistent basis with his own ideas and optimism was high at the start of Super League III, the 1998 season. Then in the Challenge Cup, magnificent performances against Leeds at Headingly and Bradford at home, gave us a tie with the Sheffield Eagles, and as Wigan found out, taking them for granted resulted in getting our backsides kicked. It still rankles with me to this day; we should not have lost at home in the third round of the cup to anyone.

Through the season, our league form was a bit inconsistent. On our travels, we notched up victories against Salford, London and Huddersfield plus a draw at St Helens, in which I scored a hat trick, whilst at home we beat Sheffield, Hull and Warrington, did the double over Salford and London, but best of all was victory over Leeds, 22-16. We finished the season in sixth place, much better than the previous year, but we were all a bit disappointed to just miss out on the play-offs. The year closed with no silverware but the promises of better things to come were hovering around Wheldon Road. Things were definitely changing, Super League was becoming firmly established and within a couple of years, the profile had lifted beyond my wildest dreams, and with astute marketing Castleford's profile rocketed - Tiger mania was catching on.

For the 1999 season Darren Rogers joined us from Salford, Michael Eager from Warrington, James Pickering from Canterbury and in a very astute move by Stuart Raper, he signed his brother Aaron from Parramatta. Personally I feel this particular season has to go down as one of the biggest in my career, it was also pretty special for Castleford as a club, if only for finally laying the Wigan ghost to rest.

We had started off the campaign with a narrow 12-10 win at home to Wakefield then achieved draws at home against Leeds and Bradford but best of all in April we resoundingly beat Wigan away, 24-8, and if that wasn't good enough, we again beat them at home, 33-18. Then after a victory against Huddersfield in our last match, we made the play-offs, finishing in fifth spot.

Our first play-off eliminator was against none other than Wigan, away at the JJB stadium. Many pundits doubted our chances of making it three in a row but we took strength from our two earlier victories and went into the match in confident mood. We won out 14-10 and our victory sent shock waves around the league, the third time in a season we had beaten them and we were on a high, but as subsequent events were to prove, it was probably the catalyst for Stuart Raper's eventual departure to our bitter red rose enemy.

Coming from fifth spot to the final eliminator against St Helens was I believe a greater achievement than making the Premiership final at Old Trafford in 1994, although losing to Saint's by a resounding

36-6 was a bitter pill to swallow. But I was a very proud man once again when chosen by my fellow players as their Player of the Year in addition I also received the coach's award. However, as always seems to have been the case during my career there would inevitably be a low to follow the high.

Stuart sang my praise for inclusion in the up and coming Tri-Nations squad tour but as before and in spite of strong support from the media and some influential people in the game, I was overlooked. Dad's and Stuart's conciliatory words were as before, telling me I could have done no more to stake my claim. But I got the impression that it wasn't just me not getting a fair crack of the whip, because although we as a team had beaten Wigan three times, not one Castleford player was included. Seven Wigan and seven Leeds players were in the squad, though I suppose the consolation was choosing a strong Castleford contingent for the Lincoln Internationals against France but it was scant reward for the months of effort, although I decided to make the best of it and I scored a try in each game, played well and enjoyed it to boot.

Playing against a well-drilled French outfit with and against some of tomorrow's stars was both enjoyable and rewarding, and as the Millennium came to a close, I often felt pangs of nostalgia over what may have been only twenty minutes against Australia at Wembley and forty minutes from the Championship Final. Then I was given my final accolade for the season by being included in the highly respected 'Rugby League Express Dream Team' at number ten.

The Millennium celebrations with its fireworks and parties came and passed and in what seemed like no time. The new season fixture lists were published, I was moving into my third decade but after our previous strong campaign and another chance at Wembley, I was still brimming over with enthusiasm and guess who we were playing in our first fixture in Super League V? Wigan at the Jungle.

Wheldon Road had been dropped as our venue name, gone was Classy Cas and the Tiger's in The Jungle were in. Our main sponsors now were Jungle.com and they helped create a high profile for the team in the world of media hype.

For me, the 1999 season had never seemed to finish, my cousin Lee and myself were still coaching Stanley Rangers, we had built a tidy squad of players and on two occasions, we had put silverware into the trophy cabinet. I was coming to the conclusion that this was where my future lay – coaching and starting out at grass roots is an ideal learning base and it kept my mind alert and body toned during the off-season. January 2000 took the Rangers to Keighley Albion in the Challenge Cup, a win here would send us into the first round, something that had never happened before in the eighty odd years of Stanley's existence. Hopes were high even though Keighley were from a higher league but the confidence we carried on to the pitch was decisive; we won and history was made.

The draw for the Challenge Cup first round was pretty much irrelevant, we were already cock-a-hoop having achieved more than we had hoped for, so it didn't really matter who would come next, but we were still delighted to get a local derby against Dewsbury. Stanley Rangers had come a long way since the amalgamation of the separate factions in the village and it was the clubs finest hour simply to go into the draw but the game proved a welcome financial boost to the coffers and also allowed young and old players, officials and fans to express themselves and laud in the occasion.

On a truly horrendous day with high winds and torrential rain, our village heroes took to the field and for the first thirty minutes we gave as good as we got. But it was inevitable that playing seasoned professionals, we would eventually tire and so it proved as Dewsbury finally ran out easy winners, 66-0.

After the match I told the lads to hold their heads up, we had fared better than most other amateur sides and I reminded them that everyone at the club was proud of them all. We then went for a celebratory drink, but I had to be careful as I had to concentrate on my game with Cas in the next round which was also against amateur opposition, from Lancashire, Oldham St Annes.

Castleford had a job to do and we approached it with exactly that attitude. I scored a hat trick and we won comfortably 64-8, but all credit to St Annes for crossing over the line, that day they were wonderful ambassadors for the game. Unfortunately they didn't acquit themselves in such a sporting manner later that season when they came up against Stanley Rangers in the quarter-finals of the National Cup. Stanley had already taken two significant scalps beating Redhill and Leigh Miners, but the game against Oldham St Annes turned spiteful and was marred by several brawls. Ranger's halfback Rob Woodcock was the victim of a stamping incident resulting in two deep cuts above his eye. Unfortunately Rob reacted which lead to his dismissal, but no action was taken against the instigator which just served to raise the already explosive atmosphere on the pitch. The referee with only a couple of minutes to go really ought to have blown time, we were 22-0 down and nothing could be gained in continuing, alas, from the restart, mayhem broke out and the game was abandoned. Stanley's subsequent financial penalty and heavy bans on two players was a massive injustice and to add insult, a video of the game that we wanted to use in evidence mysteriously disappeared. Overall, it disillusioned many within the Stanley club with what seemed a kangaroo court attitude. I was personally hurt by the obvious bias I witnessed and many of the players lost faith in BARLA. Afterwards the Stanley senior team went on a downhill slide, which they are still battling to recover from today.

As for Cas we had our millennium cup aspirations abruptly halted by Halifax at the Jungle 10-11, but we won seventeen from twenty-eight in the league to finish fifth again, however this time Leeds exacted revenge for previous shocks by beating us 22-14 in the play-off at Headingly.

At the end of the season I felt drained and was glad of the rest and I feel sure many players felt the same, the lamp oil seemed to be running low and I don't think Castleford as a club had the finances to top up the tank. And come the start of the 2001 campaign I was harbouring doubts about our squad and whether or not we were up for it. Little things, nothing you could put your finger on, but several players, me included, were carrying niggling injuries, but our new recruits arrived by March 6th and on paper we were ready to go.

For one reason or another, the season never really got going for us at Cas, there were constant rumours of Stuart Raper's impending departure then injuries to BJ Mather and Aaron Raper - it all created an undercurrent of doubt and that doesn't ever augur, well for consistent form. Then Mitch Healey picked up an injury, we were tumbled by Leeds at home in the Challenge Cup in which I was harshly sent off, and so it continued. After each knock we would re-group and try harder to match our form of the previous few seasons but then the bombshell dropped, Stuart announced he was going to Wigan! This news was hard to swallow, we had just buried the thought of him going to Cronulla so this hit home hard and brought many close to tears. Aaron also announced it was home time; he was nursing a chronic shoulder that was threatening to end his playing days. I didn't envy Graham Steadman's task when he took over.

I promised Graham I'd give him my all, after all I had seen Mal, Dad, Darryl, JJ and Stuart come and go and let's face it, it's show business and the show must go on. The upheaval obviously took its toll on the pitch but the fans stayed loyal and I achieved a few more milestones; another hat trick at Huddersfield and four hundred games for Cas. This I found particularly rewarding, becoming only the fourth player in the club's history to reach this milestone. I carried my son Joseph around the perimeter as the fans cheered and held up banners, one saying 'Another 400' which made me laugh. Joseph was in tears, I was close to tears and so were my family up in the stand. Little did I know that at that time an old mate of mine, David Nelson, who I'd played with at Cas had been callously gunned down in his local pub The Wilson Arms in Leeds. What a sad tragedy he was a really nice guy, Steady and myself attended his funeral, it was a very moving experience. I recall getting a tremendous sense of satisfaction when the police announced the apprehension of the alleged culprit; I knew that would be some sort of consolation to David's family.

Anyway, I went on to become the third highest in the appearance charts for Castleford and while I think I must have played pretty well over the years to reach such a milestone, I wonder about my abilities when compared with some of my contemporaries such as Alan Hardisty, John Joyner and Arthur Atkinson. Those players were true greats, I'd be happy just to be mentioned in years to come alongside such names, if only for the fact that I, like them was a loyal club man always determined to give my best. If some say in years to come that Diesel was a good un, then I'll be very honoured indeed.

At the time of writing this a goal I would like to achieve is that of Arthur Atkinson's 431 games before I retire, but if Steady keeps dropping me, then I'll miss out on it, well not to worry I've been dropped before, all it has done is inspire me to get back to the grindstone. I'll train harder than ever, force my way back into the side, and try to stay there.

20

Some Games Remembered

I've often been asked to name some of the games that spring to mind when reflecting back on such a long career, well the obvious ones I have already mentioned such as making my debut at Castleford, Wembley against the Aussies and with Cas, the Regal Trophy win and Yorkshire Cup final wins and losses. But I guess what is needed at this point are run of the mill league or cup games that deserve a mention because of either personal achievements or team achievements. Two that spring to mind on a personal level are firstly when we were losing at St Helens and with able assistance from Adrian Vowles, I scored a hat trick of tries in eleven minutes, I've wondered since if that has to be some sort of record for a prop? Another memorable match was when we were trailing to Huddersfield at the McAlpine Stadium and I ran in another three tries. One of these I ran down the wing and scored, maybe this is another record for a prop? But I feel I have sometimes played better or a match has been more memorable without the pleasure of scoring although my seventy plus first grade career tries is indicative that I do enjoy crossing the whitewash occasionally.

One game I recall was against Wigan during Darryl Van de Velde's reign. At half time, Darryl told me to stop running at Andy Platt all the time because he was tackling me but Andy had made that his goal early on and I responded. It was personal so I ignored Darryl's instructions and at the end of the game Andy could hardly lift either shoulder; mind you I was also sore from the encounter. That is one time Dad disagreed with Darryl, he said 'if you had gone out in the second half and started running into different channels, Andy Platt and his teammates would have been lifted'. Dad had quietly sat in the stand taking in this personal challenge and announced that it was honours even and I was correct to keep it that way to the final whistle.

Several matches at Headingley spring to mind especially during Stuart Raper's time when some real team efforts against very good Leeds sides allowed us to come out on top, like when Andrew Schick scored in the dying seconds taking a magnificent Adrian Vowles bomb, leaping like a proverbial kangaroo above everyone to take the ball and seal victory. Another time was during John Joyner's reign when I clinched my England selection against Ellery Hanley's Leeds team with me scoring the last try - probably my greatest individual performance in a Cas shirt.

Not all matches are memorable just because we won, losing to Doncaster away was a game I found difficult to swallow during their brief sojourn in Super League, not that I mean to be disrespectful to Doncaster, they were well worth the win but we went into that game expecting to turn them over. Another defeat away to Carlisle by the odd point, we had the talent to win but we did not perform and got our just deserts. But naturally it's the games we won that are more satisfying to recall and one in particular was when we beat Salford at home after losing twelve games on the trot in Super League I. This was our first positive result and provided the platform on which we avoided relegation that season.

Taking a more microscopic view of my career, playing alongside

Mal Reilly in the A-team of 1987 was very special, also our home victory over St Helens in May 2002 was a memorable occasion. Eighteen points down after fifteen minutes and then slowly getting it together, wearing them down and then winning 36-22. Leaving the pitch, I felt a real sense of satisfaction especially when seeing the reaction of the fans. Staging a comeback against such illustrious opponents, we proved that if we apply ourselves, nothing, no challenge is beyond our capabilities – I'm sure it wasn't just me taking a trip to Shangri-La after that game.

Another question often put to me is would I have preferred the old days? My dad has in the past told me my style would have suited the game in his day. I respect that opinion but would I have preferred to play then? The answer is both yes and no, I honestly believe that my disciplinary record would be much cleaner had I played then, the game was more physical and referees more relaxed. Nowadays it's the referees who complain: 'Keep those tackles down Dean.'

'But ref. I hit him in the chest.'

'I know you did but you're straying higher.'

Dad has told me in his day, if one player had discreetly given another a smack and the other later sought retribution the ref would say, 'he was only getting his own back now get on with the game. Anymore and your both off.'

I don't want to condone foul play and I endorse the modern approach to cut it out as there is no place for thugs in the game, but I just feel my disciplinary record would be deemed modest in days gone by. However, I think the downside is that because referees now have to more tightly control everything on the pitch, I believe there are less characters than there used to be – or less chance for the characters to express themselves.

If you take a look at some of today's seasoned professionals, I don't think the modern player has half as much character in his face as those of old, and that's the nicest way I can put it. I am certain it is a result of the success in tightening up the laws on foul play, thankfully players, even props, can look forward to a chance of a media career after a lifetime of rugby because they are deemed handsome and have a sexy marketable image - well enough about me! Moreover, with the financial rewards in the game today, well I would be a fool to want it to be like the past. The game is still tough but we don't want it as tough as the old days, the game still requires all the old attributes; speed, strength, power, vision, courage and craft. For better or worse, the rule changes have altered the game, and nowadays I believe it is collectively faster although individually, players who could run in 1930 may well have been as quick as their modern counterparts and the same goes for all the other attributes. Nevertheless, I think whichever era a player played or a supporter watched we should deem ourselves very lucky to be involved with such a tremendous game and I sincerely hope that in say one hundred years my descendants are still playing and possibly writing a book about their topsy-turvy careers in rugby league.

21

A Bad Day at the Office

It's a common statement made these days and often uttered by the losing coach or captain of a team, but it could also be applied to a disciplinary meeting in Leeds at Red Hall or Chapletown Road. Coming out of these meetings a player will be either smiling with a not guilty verdict or SOS (sending off sufficient), or emerge with a downcast depression and maybe the comment; 'a bad day at the office', followed by 'there's just no consistency'. Well my opinion is that this is one of the biggest problems in rugby league - consistency at all levels, but especially in refereeing and the disciplinary. I personally have consistently pleaded that I am not, and never have been, a dirty player. Of my ten dismissals in fifteen years, I was found not guilty in one, in another the verdict was NFA (no further action), where the committee felt I was technically guilty but that the offence warranted no more than a penalty, three were deemed sending off sufficient because they were minor offences leaving five others. One of these was the Mark Preston incident, which has already been explained in this book, leaving four, two of which were in 1987 and 1991 for which I received two and six match suspensions. The ninth one was the Willie Poaching incident in which I retaliated, after Willie felled Brad Davis. I do not condone what I did and I hold my hand up and admit I was very wrong and I apologised to Willie and the public at the time.

My tenth was for felling Adrian Lam when we played Wigan in July 2002.

Now referee Robert Connelly sent me from the field of play for punching three times in a ten-month period. The first time was away at Bradford in April 2000, then at home to Wakefield three months later and finally at home to Leeds the following February. I was guilty once and in the other two incidents I retaliated, now that's hardly consistent form apart from he was consistently sending me off. Contrast that with when we played the Aussie Challenge competition in 1997 when an Aussie prop punched me and I fell over my prostrate teammate. I quickly jumped to my feet and slugged him back as hard as I could. I didn't start it but I finished it and we were both sent to the sin bin to cool down for ten minutes and when I returned to the fray I never saw my opponent again. Well if the ref thought we should go to the bin then okay, I'll go along with that but I have three dismissals on my disciplinary for punching of which two are not justified.

Another referee who deserves a mention is David Campbell after he sent me off three times in consecutive seasons, 1995, 1996 and 1997, now those are consistent numbers! But two occasions were for punching or throwing a punch, of which one didn't even connect, the other was an eightieth minute tap on Steve McNamara for sledging me. I honestly believe they were not sending off offences and if Bob Connelly and David Campbell had not been referees or had been at other matches, then my previous nine dismissals would have been only four.

In the final incident against Wigan, I had taken the decision to drop me to the bench on the chin. I had trained hard and was eagerly looking forward to the game, but being told I was subbing disappointed me so I vowed if I got on the pitch I would make them sit up and take notice, at least that was my intention, and when we ran up a 10-0 lead I was even more enthusiastic. It's very frustrating sat on the bench and then to see Cas visibly wilt as Wigan began to aggressively work their way back with some dubious high shots from Terry Newton and Craig Smith which simply went unpunished. Well, as each minute passed I expected to be sent into the fray, but this was not to be and I retired into the dressing room at half-time very frustrated that my coach had felt me unworthy of a run on. But then relief and relish when I was told to get ready for the second-half. I don't like subbing or being subbed, Stuart Raper was aware of this and he gave me my head and got the best out of me but it was different this time around, Graham Steadman was trying to phase me out, understandably because I had announced my intention to retire at the end of the season. Anyway, I desperately wanted involvement and a regular comprehensive input, I felt so fit and enthusiastic and wanted to finish the season on a high note, so when I ran out for my stint I wanted to make an impact.

Wigan took up the initiative in the second-half as if there had been no interval and I soon realised it was much hotter than being on the bench. We were soon 10-16 down and Adrian Lam was running riot just as he had been in the first-half. We had agreed before the game and at half-time that he must not be allowed the freedom to dictate the pattern of the game. Now believe me when I say I did not go out looking for Adrian Lam, my mind was instantly preoccupied in stemming the Wigan tide and trying to play my own game, however circumstances prevailed that by me being busy and so too Adrian, our paths would inevitably cross, and we did with a bang!

I was late and high but my arm was bent and relaxed and it was not, I repeat not, malicious. I believe my body impact shook him more than my arm and I take this opportunity now to apologise to him.

I felt frustrated afterwards, especially being condemned by all and sundry. Dad says I'm too clumsy to play dirty, he maintains I have a sense of timing likened to Virgin Rail but he accepts that it was not malicious. I hope others eventually do too. One thing the event certainly did do was with only nine games left and a six match ban, it meant Arthur Atkinson's record number of appearances were safe. The irony of it all was Adrian Lam turned out a few days hence and once again ran rings around the opposition, had I meant to hurt him he would not have played for a long time.

So back to consistency, I don't envy Stuart Cummings his new job, it's a mammoth task with tremendous responsibilities and far reaching ramifications. Greg McAllum the previous incumbent at headquarters thought Karl Kirkpatrick's work policing the ten-metre rule was the best in the game whereas Stuart Raper's thoughts on Karl's policing were scathing, publicly complaining that with Karl in charge games would inevitably be high scoring ones. Now this leads me to throw open a poser - was Stuart Cummings given the Challenge Cup final as a sentimental leaving present? If so fine, I can live with that, but we all know from our Semi against Wigan and the Saints final, that the teams were on top of each other in both games and there were very few free kicks, less than eight in total for both games. I know coaches will want consistency but will it be Stuart Cummings version of consistency? Will he stamp the rules as they are written or how he thinks a game should flow because it defies the law of probability that four teams in two such important encounters with so much at stake should make so few transgressions of the laws? I look forward in keen anticipation of what is to come as I too move into the coaching office and I sincerely hope that the adage 'a bad day at the office' is heard to be quoted less by one and all.

22

Headingly Revisited

The semi-final of the Challenge Cup is either a magical or a traumatic time for any player and recently I have enjoyed the pleasure and suffered the traumas associated with such occasions. Most players will concur, even overseas players agree, that the aura of this competition is unsurpassed anywhere in the world and when you reach the semi, you're fully aware that you are only eighty minutes from Wembley, or in more recent times, Murrayfield, Twickenham or Cardiff. But the semi-final is the worst stage in the competition to lose, believe me it hurts far more than the final because then you've at least had the pleasure of savouring the occasion, the pomp and ceremony. But don't get me wrong, defeat in the final is an awful experience, it's just that to lose a semi takes much more out of you psychologically, you are drained, you feel empty and it has a bigger impact on the next few games you play - at least that is how I found it. And if it's a controversial loss, then it becomes a double whammy, 'IF ONLY' becomes magnified, and while the winners leave the field in high spirits on the way to Wembley, the losers have only their ill luck or mistakes or the controversial to fall back on.

In 1999 Castleford played the London Broncos at Headingley, the game had swung too and fro at a frenetic pace but I felt it was game over when with only eight minutes left, Michael Eager scored a superb try, Cas taking the lead 27-24. I was making my way back to the half way line with visions of the final firmly implanted in my thoughts, a dream come true. Stuart Raper signalled me to come off, my wind and my legs were fine but I had injured my hand, which was heavily strapped, so it never dawned on me to protest. My dad was sat in the stand, and my sister Becky told me later that he had buried his head in his hands uttering, 'no, no Dean, tell Stuart you want to stay on, you're only eight minutes from Wembley, it's not over yet'. I still respect his perception of the game to this day. Anyway, that was the controversy, I don't blame Stuart, neither does Dad, it's just that he had always prescribed that a player knows best in such circumstances. I was an experienced player, I was playing well and my teammates needed me for those last few vital minutes. Maybe he was flattering me that I and I alone would be the difference but with hindsight I should have asked Stuart to leave me on the field, at least he would have had the chance to consider subbing someone else. But I didn't protest, then London played a short kick-off, gained possession and we were on the back foot. London scored and the rest is history, I was sat on the bench and it didn't sink in at first, but as the days passed it aggrieved me more but I put it down to a good lesson learned.

I suppose one good thing that came from that semi-final defeat was it inspired me to play for a few more years as I had been planning to retire at the end of the season, so dad negotiated a new contract for me. Well the old adage of history repeating itself came true, when in 2002, we made the semi-final once again at Headingley, but this time we faced the mighty Wigan. Into the second half, we were 14-10 down - it was nip and tuck, Graham Steadman was now my coach and my old mentor Stuart Raper was in charge at Wigan. Graham brought me off early in the second half. 'Have a rest; I'll put you back on later.'

Now I was three years older, I had topped the tackle count and was glad of a breather but I still felt strong and was happy knowing I was going to get another crack before long. But it wasn't to be, Graham told me to warm up, the clock was ticking down and the score was still 14-10. I was ready to go on but it didn't happen then in the dying seconds, Gary Connolly forced his way over and Wigan were on their way to Murryfield with a 20-10 victory. To a man we had given our all throughout the club but Wigan were worthy opponents, and they also got the rub of some refereeing decisions, though in this case I thought Stuart Cummings being praised in one newspaper for only giving four penalties was pushing credibility a bit too far. Neither side conceded an offside penalty and only one at the play the ball against me that was proven incorrect on video, making three transgressions. If those were the facts then the rugby paper should have been praising the two teams and not the ref.

With so much at stake, while I was disappointed for myself I was pleased for Stuart given it was intimated he was under pressure in his job. I think it's fair to say he's turning things around at Wigan and the fact that he had taken them to a Challenge Cup final in his second season at the club underlines his ability. And if he is allowed reasonable time I'm sure he will make Wigan once again a dominant force in rugby league, but if he's not then I believe it will be their loss.

23

The Highs and Lows on the Ladder of Life

Everyone has highs and lows in life and for me personally, apart from getting married, the birth of my kids, the death of my granddad and other family matters, they have tended to revolve around my playing career. But I acknowledge I've been lucky not only in being able to enjoy playing professional rugby but also because my dad and my coaches helped me understand the psychology of the ladder of life.

Now throughout my playing career I have found that the ladder of life is a bloody long ladder indeed and I'm only glad that the people around me weren't firemen because it may have been longer still. But anyway, once you get up to the top, it's a beautiful view, but then you have to go back to the bottom as the ladder moves from site to site, offering you a fresh challenge each time. I now have a foot on the coaching ladder, taking charge of the Castleford Academy side and the challenge for me now is to once again climb to the top. But I take this opportunity to give you, the reader, an insight to the highs and lows on my ladder of life throughout my playing career:

Highs	Lows
Signing professional forms for Castleford.	Being told by Dad that I had one foot on a new ladder but it was the bottom rung.
Getting the Man of the Match award in the A-team Yorkshire Cup final.	Dad saying that Johny Milner was his choice.
Getting the A-team Player of the Year award.	Being told by Dad he was proud, 'but you have only moved up one rung'.
My first team debut (a try and a win).	The first time I was relegated to sub.
Alliance Player of the Year again plus twenty-three first team games, ten played, thirteen at sub.	Dad telling me to set my sights higher and that I was only on the the third rung.
Being selected for the under-21 international and scoring a try.	Being told by Dad that he played on the wing against France for his country but never represented them again.
A Yorkshire Cup winner's medal at the third attempt and voted Man of the Match by my fellow players.	Dad saying that it was just one game and that he'd be impressed if I received the Player's Player for a full season.
Sweeping the board at the end of season awards including Player's Player, Coach's Player and First Team Player.	Dad telling me he was very proud, 'you are halfway up the ladder'.

At this stage in my career I began to wonder about this so-called ladder, how long was it and where was it leading? So I asked, 'hey Dad, how long is this ladder?'

'Ask your Uncle Malcolm Son, he'll tell you.'

The next time I sat down for a drink with Uncle Malcolm, I popped the question. 'How long is the ladder of life that Dad says I'm on?'

'Oh that'll be a pole ladder Dean, longest one you can get in the building trade, it'll take you right to the apex of the gable end, when you get to the top of that ladder your ready for putting the roof on, why do you ask? How far does your dad say you've got?'

'He says I'm only halfway up.'

'Well, I reckon that's about right.' He replied.

So the highs and lows of my ladder of life continued:

Highs	Lows
Tipped to tour in the Summer of 1990 after a thirty-four game season.	Being told by Mal Reilly I wasn't going.
Going to Australia and playing with Gold Coast Seagulls.	Not being able to stay because of the new overseas draft system.
Winning the Yorkshire Cup for a second time and playing a thirty-five game season.	Not being chosen against the Aussies.
Getting to Wembley in the Challenge Cup final.	Losing the Challenge Cup final to Wigan.
Winning the Regal Trophy against Wigan.	Losing to Wigan in the Challenge Cup semi-final.
Getting to the Championship final at Old Trafford.	Losing to Wigan by four points and being cited.
Playing against the Aussies at Cas and getting the Man of the Match.	Losing the Regal Trophy semi-final against Wigan.
Being chosen in the World Cup squad and finally representing my country as a full international.	Missing out on a World Cup final appearance.
Finally getting a Great Britain jersey against the Aussies.	Not getting another chance for Great Britain because of an ankle injury.
Having a testimonial granted.	Not having a successful testimonial.
Sweeping the board once again in the Player of the Year awards and receiving The Past Players Association award.	Losing the Challenge Cup 1999 and 2002 semi-finals.
Being told by Dad I was on the top rung of the ladder.	Getting a six-match ban in my final season.
Playing over 400 games for Castleford and achieving third place in the club records for games played.	Retiring from the professional game.
Turning out for my beloved Stanley Rangers.	Being sent off for the first time as an amateur.

24

Opinions

A question I'm often asked is, 'are rugby players nowadays fitter than before?' Well seeing as sixteen years have elapsed since I turned professional and I've played in pre and present Super League, I feel perfectly entitled to offer not only an opinion but a reasoned argument and I will try to use players I have known to make comparisons. Take for instance Cas training sessions in Pontefract Park, if the order of the day was a one lap two-and-a-half mile run or a two lap 5 mile run, I cannot think of any modern player who would beat either David Rookley or Bob Beardmore in their prime. And if you compared a short sprint, well, Bob Beardmore was like a whippet, although Dad would argue no quicker than Alan Hardisty. On a longer distance sprint, say over a 100 metre dash, John Joyner was quick and so too Fizzer Fenton. In the gym and callisthenics, Tony Marchant was very special, a true competitor, equal in his prime to any professional today. And a weights session with Mal Reilly and Kevin Ward must have been on a par with any rugby athlete in the whole world then and now. No, the only thing that's different today is that players generally stay fitter for longer due to training, medical and dietary advances. Players today are also helped by rule changes and I don't believe that some of them are for the better, for instance, I think we should bring back competing scrums, forwards will tire quicker and it will also make them play the ball correctly, it's farcical and inconsistent at the moment.

Whilst in a reflective mood, I asked Dad for his thoughts on rugby league today; he argued, 'the game needs to find some useful paid employment for some of the former greats like John Joyner and David Topliss. Players like these have so much to offer so they should be given positions in the development and coaching of the Conference League teams and that's the way to develop our game. Fast tracking does not work, whether it is Gateshead or Wales. For Gods sake, it doesn't take the Brain of Britain to know this is the way forward, hundreds of kids are taking to the game of rugby league because it's a joy to play and these latter day converts are the future.'

I'm inclined to agree that Dad has a point, I wonder how many former players are lost to the game on retirement, hundreds each year I suspect. He always gives me food for thought does my dad.

Occasionally professional players will get together over a beer and have a reflective conversation about the game, we all have our opinions and a collective affinity as to how it should be played and how the rules are interpreted by different referees and even different hemispheres. I personally believe, as I have mentioned elsewhere, that our refereeing standards could be better. But don't misunderstand me, I appreciate that a ref has a hard and thankless task and I'm sure we all agree on that, however, the truth of the matter is that some referees that have recently been fast tracked to the top are just woeful – understandably when you consider the experience they're lacking. But this in turn has far reaching ramifications to the progress and quality of our game in comparison to say Australia, where they are becoming more than ever clinically correct in every aspect of their game. For example, we now see referees over in Aus penalising offside at kick-offs, which was unheard of in the last fifty years. It may seem pedantic but they are deliberately tidying all the loose ends of apparent incorrectness. Another area is at the play the ball. I have noticed a concentrated effort on their part to speed up this aspect of the game to the point where Bill Harrigan, probably the top Aussie whistler, sin-binned four Parramatta players for play the ball offences. In this case, Bill's overzealousness earned him a downgrading, but don't think for one minute the policing won't continue.

Now all these things were apparent leading up to and during our recent ill-fated one-off test. In hindsight everyone agrees it was a mistake to arrange a game like that, but I know of people who were predicting the outcome before the event and not in a cynical or negative way, but because they had the necessary foresight - some of our so called old brigade, the discarded ones.

Also a contentious issue was the choice of referee. My understanding of the situation is that we agreed to Bill Harrigan doing the final test in the previous series so that we could take our ref over for this one-off test match. Well big deal, they already knew it was going to be Russell Smith and that suited them just fine. Now Russell is a good ref and ultra fair, he maintains a consistent ten metres and most importantly, he is strong at the play the ball. These three things made Russell more than acceptable to the Aussies; we already knew that they were faster, bigger and stronger so Russell was the final piece to compliment their strategy. But the irony of it is that our people were believing it a coup in our favour! If we are ever to beat the old enemy, or even New Zealand for that matter, then I reckon we need to call on a couple of seasoned poker players to assist a new long term strategic game plan that we must think out for ourselves and implement by ourselves. Then maybe we can cease being simply a satellite extension of Australian and Sky expansionism of their version of rugby league. We should be involving some of our past greats directly at the hub of our game, ex-players with keen minds, like Reilly, Hardisty, Hepworth, Gregory, Edwards, Hanley and Murphy. People who have proved their ability both on and off the field. They should be working directly with the administrators and the up and coming players and coaches to drive the game forward at both domestic and international level. Then maybe, just maybe, we'll start to see the tables turned on the old enemy from down under.

25

The Westgate Run

I answered my mobile at around two o'clock in the afternoon; it was cup final day, another Murryfield spectacular in the offing. Dad was on the other end of the phone. 'We are in The Redoubt, are you and Jonty coming down?'

'Yes, Uncle Malcolm is joining us as well.' I replied.

The plan had been to meet in Wakefield further up Westgate, possibly at The White Hart. Dad, Big Mack and Melvin Castle had started an hour earlier, the change of plan made no difference Uncle Malcolm preferred the beer at The Redoubt anyway, not that he'd ever been in The White Hart. We arrived twenty minutes later and managed to squeeze in the back room where the TV was situated. The atmosphere was just right, family and friends and a few pub regulars, the beer was spot on and Uncle Malcolm's first pint soon vanished. 'Like wine.' He exclaimed as he passed over his empty pot.

'Who do you fancy Dean?' Big Mack asked.

'Wigan, Mack.' I replied, only to be drowned by boos and derisive comments followed by chants of Saints - Saints – Saints! This surprised me a little that they had decided to support St Helens for the afternoon. But my hopes were for Stuart Raper and John Kear, both had been my coaches during my career and I liked, admired and respected them. I knew Dad felt the same and as I passed a pint to Uncle

Malcolm, he proffered his opinion to the same question to him from Mack. 'I don't give a chuff as long as it's a good game.' As always, he was straight to the point

It was national anthem time and as the opening bars sounded, Big Mack rose from his stool to stand to attention alone. Amongst the hubbub, Scott stole his seat and passed it to Mel who in turn put it behind the door as the last note faded and the stadium erupted into wild waving and enthusiastic cheering. Our own little band were equally switched on to the event and there was a unified burst of laughter as Big Mack who had switched up the volume then turned to sit down. 'Where's my bloody stool, who's pinched my bloody seat? Come on you bastards give it back.'

Mel gave in and passed the buffet over from behind the door and innocently proclaimed, 'hey Mack there's a spare one here'.

Mack sat and settled mumbling to himself as the shrill sound of the whistle of Stuart Cummings started the game. This inspired an immediate comment from Scott. 'What's he doing refereeing? He was crap in the semi-final.'

Mel concurred nodding his head like a toy dog. 'You're right, gave Wigan eight points start he did.'

Then Uncle Malcolm interjected. 'They look at the video replay for a try but they should do so for a penalty as well.'

'Yes but the game would be stop and start.' Mack replied.

'Cummings only gave four penalties all game so it wouldn't take that long.'

Dad then made his usual profound input. 'If he only gave four penalties and the video proved he got one drastically wrong then that's a twenty-five percent failure rate, so how the hell did he get this final over Russell Smith?'

Oohs and ahs were in abundance as the game ebbed and flowed. Then Mel took up the chair. 'Russell Smith didn't get it and Cummings did because Cummings is one of Maurice's men.'

Suddenly Mack wanted to know how he could know that, Mel pointed to his nose. 'I know people Mack,' then he chided, 'eh Sammy have you paid yet?' He waved an empty pint glass, three visible white froth lines indicating how many times it had been in contact with his lips.

'I got the first round in and I gave our Jonty a tenner to get the last one so it must be your turn Mack.' Dad replied.

Dad handed his glass over. 'I'll look after your stool Mack.' He dryly said, as a muttering Mack stumbled into the passage bar.

Mack re-entered the fray, four pints to hand and a pork pie in his mouth, no one noticed behind his giant frame the sylph like figure of Kaz the barmaid in his wake. She placed a sauce bottle in front of Uncle Malcolm and some serviettes together with some white plastic knives; we each exchanged quizzical glances that were soon answered by the re-appearance of Kaz with two beer trays full of whole pork pies. As she placed them down on the table, she said. 'There you are Malcolm, I knew you were the civilised one so I have made you the chef for the day, oh and big Mack has already had some.'

As Kaz turned to go, Mack barked. 'Put us some sauce on those top rollers and you can stick your pork pies.'

'Oh, why have you lost your dummy?' Kaz replied. The whole place once again erupted into laughter. Then as a parting shot, she said. 'Lowers the tone does Mack, don't you think Malcolm?'

Attention was now drawn back to the television as people shouted and cheered in favour of St Helens. Keiron Cunningham had dived under the sticks to score for Saints. Stuart Cummings called for the video ref, the replays repeated the touch down from different angles and everyone in the pub was unanimous. 'What's he waiting for, it's a try.' The fervour and frustration of a whole room of people supposedly impartial confirmed my long held opinion that rugby league fans are very passionate and loyal once they have proclaimed an allegiance. Then when Ray Tennant announced no try, Dad and Uncle Malcolm sat looking at each other with their bottom jaws dropping in disbelief. The game continued and despite the drained plastic sauce bottle becoming airborne several times, interest had waned for most, and many, probably without foundation, bandied accusations too and fro. Some questioned the video ref's parentage, others said it was Stuart Cummings fault for using the video ref and someone else shouted that both officials were Maurice Lindsay's men. Then an old wag, a well-dressed senior citizen, proclaimed that Maurice and Stuart Cummings were both Free Masons, on hearing this Mack asked Uncle Malcolm if it was true. 'How the hell should I know, I've never even met either of them before. Ask our kid Mack.' He replied.

He repeated his question and aimed it at Dad. 'Well if they do belong to a secret society it's not the Buffalos.' This statement brought a mixture of laughter and quizzical looks in Dad's direction then a bemused Big Mack put forward the inevitable. 'What the fuck is a Buffalo?'

Scott was the quickest. 'It's a hairy cow with two horns.' The place erupted in uproar as a crimson faced Mack chinned Scott for taking the piss. Mel then chimed in 'Hey Mack, Sammy's a Buffalo you know.'

All this conversation and banter taking place with craning necks facing the television, Mack then slowly turned to face his tormentors, a disdainful expression on his face, and purposefully stated. 'Well if that's the case then I agree, Sammy is hairy and horny so if the cap fits wear it.' This brought another volley of laughter as more foaming pints were placed on the table by Kaz.

The game finally arrived at its inevitable conclusion with Wigan lifting the trophy after a 21-12 victory. I felt happy for Stuart and John, the Wigan lads and Maurice but I don't think he would have appreciated the cross banter. Nevertheless, we were now embarking on the serious part of the day, the Westgate Run, the infamous trail of hostelries stretching all the way to Wakefield town centre. The conversation seemed to dwell on the controversial no try decision only intermittently broken by the unanimous agreement of the Lance Todd award to Kris Radlinski. Dad explained to Mack that the Buffalos were the poor man's secret society and we managed to make it as far as the Black Horse, eight pubs in total, we had enjoyed a great final and received wonderful hospitality from Martin and Kaz. As we said cheerio to each other, bed and a good kip were the dream topping on a fun filled day out on the Westgate Run.

26

Fingers Crossed For Justice

Dad's book, Fast Lane to Shangri-La included the story of how as a family we were made bankrupt, and explained how my sister and myself were also caught up as guarantors. Well, we have now got the first couple of years over with and my life is slowly getting back on track but not without a few scars. To have to endure what our family has been through I wouldn't wish on anyone, each of us as had to try and cope in our own and different ways, for myself I have thrown myself in to rugby once again and concentrated on the welfare of my wife and two children. My sister Rebecca had to move back in with Mum and Dad, and gave invaluable support tidying up all the inevitable loose ends but she too is now ready to emerge and rise to the new challenges that life has to offer. As for Dad, well he has his good and bad days, at fifty-seven years old he can still think a good game but he's not as fit as he would like to be and this makes his battle all the harder.

At the start of the bankruptcy when we visited the official receiver in Leeds, we immediately realised the enormity of the task in front of us. I feared we might lose our homes but Dad reassured me differently and with the help and support of my wife and her family, we have managed to secure our home. As for the businesses interests, they have simply been torn from us in a ruthless manner, all explained away as for the benefit of creditors, well one thing I have learned is that it's for the benefit of administrators costs and the preferential creditors, there will be no provision or dividend for unsecured ones. Oh no, the people dealing with the bankruptcy are ruthless and during these past months we have all suffered highs and lows, each being affected in different ways and in varying degrees.

I personally almost went over the top and nearly lost my family, my rugby, everything. However, I was fortunate that the club and officials gave me support, as did my family plus many others who all helped me pull through those dark days. At the time I was drinking as well as taking anti-depressants from the doctor, Dad ended up having to hide the capsules after one incident and I turned on him, the one and only time in my life. I dried out in Becky's room and after a long chat with Dad; I decided I had to come to terms with what was on the table for the sake of the whole family. I just had not realised that everyone was looking for a lead from me. Dad was struggling to rekindle enthusiasm and energy to cope and with me leading the way, he believed we could win the uphill battle in negotiating with the solicitors and receivers. Then Dad found sustenance in writing that resulted in the publishing of his book and he also started to write poetry on anything topical or inspirational, things that reflected his moods from day-to-day; I think it became a kind of catharsis in which he could express his feelings and relieve the stress. There have been many such poems over the months. Aunt Connie encourages Dad to compose them then Denise, Kate or Becky type them up. I have included this one in this book, which was one of the first poems Dad wrote, I think it is very profound and has been inspirational to us both at this difficult time.

Sacrifice

Men and boys would toil long days
Hewing for coal for a pittance in pay
Black gold sought, black gold gained
Knee deep in water, back wrenching pain

Further and further into the fray
Developing new faces at work night and day
Skimping on safety, the occasional prop
Fearful of shifts when roof rock would drop

Whole families buried, father with sons
Crushed lifeless limbs interred as if one
Pit props are doubled but life is still brief
Explosions and fires continue the grief

These strong brave men fought for their rights
Giving their lives yet embossed with foresight
Most mines are discarded; some cry it's a shame
Others are vengeful and seek someone to blame

But our heroes descendants, the ones who survived
Are now academics wearing badges of pride
Proud of bold ancestors who unselfish in strife
Made yesteryears sacrifice that now breaths new life.

Dad is now fighting to have the bankruptcy annulled, I'm confident
he will win through, such is his determination for justice, although we

will never get our businesses back. Dad says, 'bugger the material things, but your name and pride does not have a price that can be put on it.'

Despite the traumas of this period in our lives, I'm now philosophical about the future, together with my wife we are working hard to give our two children a solid base to grow from and thankfully Mum and my sister Becky act as baby-sitters when needed. We all try to give Dad our unflinching support as he continues to battle the injustice that has befallen our family since March 2001. And just as I did with my business interest, I'm trusting Dad to fight on all our behalves and the fact that he almost daily reports some progress or a set back is representative of the time consuming battle he is having with trustees, receivers and solicitors. He tells me; no he assures me we will win, we will get justice. I hope he is right; especially when he explains things like the banks receiver has sold my pub off for £135,000 when it was already up for sale at the time of the bankruptcy for £235,000. It all takes some comprehending. We knew from the new owners of the pub that a phone call from the receiver had assured them it was a snip and totally ignoring protocol and protests by Dad to the trustee, the sale was railroaded through. For this service, the appointed receiver charged £11,000 plus agent and solicitors fees on top. And if that wasn't a rip-off, the sale of Samson's our flagship pub in Stanley was an even more bitter pill to swallow. We paid £180,000 in 1991 invested a further £70,000 then had it valued in 2000 at £280,000. This same receiver sold it for £80,000 on the instructions from the brewery. Now he will take his charges from that £80,000 but the double whammy is that the brewery then come back to the trustee for what they claim is a shortfall of £20,000 on the Railway and about £150,000 on Samson's. But I guess what rankles most is these leeches expect myself and Dad to just roll over and go away, don't make any waves; well there's a tsunami on the way and we're following in the lead canoe!

Our understanding is that over £200,000 was offered for Samson's and £222,000 for the Railway, yet the so-called professional and his agents raised the grand total of £215,000 for both properties - less expenses of course!

The conclusion, the sting that has been perpetrated, is policed by no one. The trustee won't use funds he is holding to take part in this cockfight, he's keeping what he has for his own expenses. He is not going to risk litigation, and we can't take legal action, we are not allowed to because we're bankrupt and the creditor can't because they are not aware. Only when each receives a communication from the trustee explaining that no dividend will be paid are they made aware and then it's too late, the poor old creditor probably blames us. Well that's why we are not rolling over and going away; Dad is fighting a battle that can be likened to D'Artagnan holding six of Cardinal Richelieu's men at bay, climbing staircases and swinging from chandeliers, and as in the films he'll come out smiling and winning, for we still believe in 'all for one and one for all'. It's a pity some of our so-called friends don't share this sentiment.

Recently Dad told me of a trip to Preston to see the creditor's solicitor. It had been he who made Dad and myself bankrupt on behalf of the creditor, but we had maintained dialogue with him because of his sympathetic attitude. His opening statement when Dad spoke with him. 'If I had been your solicitor neither of you would have been made bankrupt.' He then proceeded to go through his file and agreed to allow us to photocopy all of the relevant documents, which together with his statement, confirmed what we had alleged, that we should never have been made bankrupt. When this evidence was sent to our new solicitor in Leeds, Dad and I were called in and given the news that in his opinion we had a case. He also confirmed he was in agreement with the creditor's solicitor that if he had been handling our case two years previously, the bankruptcies would have been prevented. He said to us. 'If you had come to me with this case, Clause 375 of the Insolvency Law quite clearly states that if secured equity is offered then the bankruptcy application would have been denied.'

'But the creditor agreed to take the security offered, there was no argument.' Dad replied.

Steve our solicitor then continued. 'A competent solicitor would have wrapped everything up in a few hours, if only you had come to me early, I am sure with these facts I could have got it annulled.'

Dad explained he did not have the facts back then; the details were only recently given to him by another solicitor who had read his book and contacted him to confirm this injustice should not be swept under the carpet. Then Dad asked, 'where do we go from here?'

'Well, as much as I sympathise and I'm sure a judge would also, I doubt we will get an annulment now, but I'll make some enquiries and if it looks like you stand a chance then we'll sue instantly for gross negligence, if not we can talk to your trustee. It's all very complicated so we must choose the right option and not let sentiment and pride cloud our judgement, take a few days to think it over.'

Afterwards Dad and I talked about the options and the complexities, he then asked for my opinion. I felt drained, I realised we were winning the war but there was still a long way to go so I must be patient get on with my life and keep faith, plus my fingers crossed in the British justice system.

To think I almost lost faith in Dad a couple of weeks ago but I should not have and hopefully, through his efforts, we can get an annulment soon. His stubborn resolve in refusing to roll over and fade into the background has brought him and our family within sight of a new start. Whether or not we win the battle in the end remains to be seen but I'm backing Dad as he fights on to the bitter end, driven on by the innate determination shown by his father and his father before him.

A positive outcome from all this turmoil is Dads newly discovered ability for writing. As I mentioned earlier, he has started expressing his feelings in poetry and he is also now on his third book - a must for all Cas fans the biography of Kevin Ward. I'm sure the Saints fans and those in Manly, Australia, will enjoy it too. He recently told me he has entered two of his poems into a poetry competition and then he dropped a real bombshell when he calmly announced that he's cut a record, a song called 'In Your Dreams You'll Fly'. I asked him what market he's aiming for. 'Anyone who appreciates melody and a sing-a-long.' He replied.

Apparently, Aunt Connie loves it, so before long all the housewives around the country will be humming and singing along.

'It will make us rich, so you could be my bodyguard and I'll have loads of screaming fifty-year-old fans after me.' He said.

Mum butted in. 'They can have you delivered dear!'

'Now don't get jealous it's just part of being a pop star, I'm sure it will be tiresome but you will just have to live with it.'

'Yes and you'll have to take our Becky along just to clip those wings that take you on those bloody flights in your dreams,' Mum retorted, 'it's no wonder I haven't been able to sleep you must have been flapping your arms about all night flying from pillar to post.'

This was becoming a one sided contest and Dad gracefully sank his head into the paper mumbling inaudibly so I took the opportunity and bid them both farewell with a smile and a laugh.

As I drove away I tried once again to digest and comprehend exactly where my future lay and what it held for me, I reflected that life has not been easy for us of late, a seemingly never ending series of events causing me to have mood swings and fits of depression. Sometimes at a moment of impulsiveness I would hit the bottle - and not just one, seeking solace for my problems but I can now quite categorically state that it does not work, you can be as fit-as-a-fiddle, strong-as-an-ox but the combination of a weak mind, a state of depression and alcohol are a toxic mix spelling inevitable disaster. Alcohol only exacerbates the problem; it can make wimps believe they are Superman so imagine what it can do to a trained athlete. Thankfully, that stage is behind me and I hope I'm now setting a lead and becoming the inspiration to my charges at the Cas Academy.

27

Don't Stoke the Boiler!

As I write this chapter, it's nearing the end of Super League VII and I've just endured a frustrating enforced layoff due to a six week ban. On the positive side, it has allowed me to have treatment on a few niggling injuries and helped my body to recharge but alas, there are only three games remaining, unless we make the top six and the play-offs. It's at times like this when it hits home that I feel I have let down the Cas fans, my coach and team mates, and whilst a £400 fine doesn't sound too much, it is a bitter pill when you add the loss of six match monies at a time when I can ill afford it.

My old mentor Stuart Raper's complaints about me worked, but it seems ironic that I didn't hear him make any comments about Martin Gleeson trying to bite Jamie Ainscough's arm off in the Wigan-Saints game. Gleeson missed the following game because of dental damage, Ainscough in time will return home to Australia with broken bits of tooth embedded in his forearm, which no doubt will occasionally make their way to the surface like bits of shrapnel. He'll be able to reflect that even the eagle-eyed media and disciplinary panels all for some reason turned a blind eye to the contender in the 'Most Malicious Tackle of the Year to go Unpunished awards'. Then further ironies as Craig Greenhill sends Troy Slattery into temporary inactivity and gets a paltry one match ban, David Furner and John Stankevitch swop punches - several of them and receive a wag of the finger, Barrie McDermott and Saint Stuart Fielden swop blows and Barrie Mac gets four games plus a £500 fine. In my eyes Saint Stuart retaliated, he threw the ball away in retaliation to aggression and thus played his part in the incident, but no action was taken against him. I did a crime, I'll do my time, but no one can ever convince me that justice is being seen to be done.

The feedback I get in my village is one of sheer frustration at having watched all these events live and on TV, followed by total inconsistency in dealing with each incident. After all, it seems a couple of punches by two Aussie props in Sydney is called gaining each others respect and yet over here it's either ignored or the book is thrown at you. All rugby players and fans ask for is consistency – we all know it's a tough game so why does everyone panic? Have we created a pressure cooker syndrome that we are finding difficult to live with? Club chairman with a vested interest, referees unsure and leaderless coaches appointed then sacked at a whim? How on earth did David Plange have a chance at Warrington? If he's not the man for the job now after only a few months in charge, then he wasn't the man when they gave him the job, he certainly has my sympathy as does Peter Roe at Wakefield.

What I ask happens to my mate Adrian Vowles if Wakefield who have flirted with relegation for several seasons, finally go down - is that another coaching team to be culled? At least if I make the grade in coaching, I'll be going in with my eyes open. I'm ambitious to get to the top in this chosen field and I'm fully aware of the pitfalls, but I'll not can my forthright views nor will I cow-tow to convention for I believe only the innovative, ambitious and passionate stand a chance of surviving the merry-go-round in the future of our sport.

Mixed emotions, that's how I can explain my feelings regarding my last home game for Castleford on Sunday September 15th. Our opponents were Widnes and the vital prize for winning would be to keep our hopes alive of the coveted sixth position. A loss and the trip to Salford would be meaningless, apart from helping Wakefield if they happened to beat Warrington and Halifax. Following my six game ban I had returned against Warrington the previous week from the bench, we were behind but I was up for it when I went on. Then a raised elbow from Nick Fozzard caught me in the throat and I reacted with a single blow, stupid but understandable given that we prop's are expected to keep the boilers stoked for the rest of the lads. A penalty was given away but honour maintained, but little did I realise that come half-time my coach would let me know his feelings in no uncertain terms and I was limited as to how much contribution I would make in the second half by having my run on time curtailed. Then as the following week progressed I began to believe I was going to be left out of the team altogether for the Widnes game, so naturally I was concerned. However, I was relieved when Graham named me at sub after insisting that I must not under any circumstances give away penalties, no late miss-timed tackles, no retaliation, no dissent - in other words go into the engine room but don't stoke the boiler. I agreed to his terms and was rewarded with a bench spot.

Half-time in the Widnes game came then Graham put me on for the second stanza, I must admit I was keen to impress as I always find watching from the sidelines frustrating, but more so today nearing the end of my last season and my 427th first team appearance.

The weather was fine and sunny with a healthy shirt sleeved crowd in attendance. The first half had been intense without too much controversy, Cas defensively had dominated and were leading but the game was far from over. We kicked off and I soon slotted into the rhythm and speed of the game, Widnes seemed a little more fired up this half or was it my imagination - it's always difficult to make comparisons from the bench. Then we went further ahead with a try from Andy Johnson and the temperature began to increase as Widnes were not going to lie down. I assumed Neil Kelly had given them a rallying call at half-time because they came back at us. We were just inside our own half when I moved out and enveloped myself around Troy Stone as he was driving in. I jumped to my feet unaware that anything was amiss as Troy began to rise, however, I was in for a surprise he simply released the ball and set about me with a concerted attack of punches, first one on the chin then three more to the forehead. I recall that the only thing going through my mind was I promised Steady, so I turned away fully expecting this to bring things to a conclusion, but no, Troy hit me another two times to the jaw from the back and then I was told a hay-maker to the back of my head. I looked at Stone; he was certainly upset about something. The referee, Richard Silverwood consulted his two linesmen and gave a penalty to us, he then pulled me over and said, 'Dean, look don't get drawn into anything or start fighting.' I thought that's rich, not one word to Troy Stone, the crowd seemed incensed even more by this and suddenly the Jungle was white hot. I gave instructions that from the resultant penalty, I was taking the next drive and I did from the next play and instantly another ruckus broke out, another melee that had Richard Silverwood not bottled out a few seconds previously would not have happened. Daniel Frame was sin-binned and once again, I just walked away. Steady decided to blood-bin me and I returned to the fray a few minutes before the end.

It was a sweet victory, more so that it was Widnes as I had almost signed for Neil Kelly the previous summer until Cas came with an offer of another season. Anyway, the fight for a play-off place was still on and the trip to Salford still proved an incentive. But the scenes at the end of this last home game will live with me forever, several thousand remained to cheer the team, Richard Gay who was also retiring received a great ovation, as for me, well nothing was going to spoil my day, not Widnes or Troy Stone or anyone else. Graham Steadman said he was proud of me for showing such restraint and allowing myself to become a human punch bag, I reminded him, 'only this once and never again'. Luck had it that my five-year old son Joseph hits harder than Troy Stone or I might have suffered some damage.

The irony of it all is had I struck back and connected, he would have gone to hospital and I would have been sent off. I didn't retaliate and he wasn't marched, I won't lose any sleep over the incident but perhaps some questions, serious questions, need addressing. I mean, who picks such an inexperienced young ref for a vital game? But the bigger moral dilemma comes from the fact that two respected coaches differ so alarmingly as to what is and what isn't expected of a front rower in the modern game.

Having seen Darryl Powell on TV so honestly and passionately defend Barrie McDermott in the infamous Stuart Fielden incident and contrast what he expects of his prop, his enforcer, with my own coach Graham Steadman who demands a more disciplined approach. Well, if Stuart Raper curtailed the aggression of his front three of Smith, Newton and O'Conner, I don't think Wigan would have enjoyed their success this season without the raw aggression to create a platform on which Adrian Lam and Julian O'Neil could invoke their silky skills.

I was disappointed that Neil Kelly had said that it was no coincidence that the game had deteriorated on my introduction and said nothing to justify his own player's reaction. Had it happened in my street, well common assault or GBH would have been the prosecution. Last year my dad got two years probation for giving an upstart a smack. I'm not whinging about Stone's attack on myself, just the inconsistency of the adjudicators in the game and the inability to approach sport and life on a level playing field. Referees, coaches, the hierarchy and the fans should all be pulling in the same direction, it is no less than our great game deserves. By the way Troy got one match, if that had been me it would probably have been four to six.

28

The Fat Jap

The inception of Super League and with it summer rugby finished an end-of-season ritual, or it certainly did at Cas, a small town club, lots of local players, a true community sprit throughout the team. Every year in late May we would all meet at the ground then board a coach to the airport for the end of season break. These trips varied between Tenerife, Magaluf and Benidorm, usually arrived at with a democratic vote. Now this particular trip would be the last under the old league, in future it would take place in November, so we all set off for Magaluf with suitcase in one hand and a drink in the other. This would be my eighth visit to this Mediterranean oasis, the drinks trolley on the plane continually ran out of cans and the hostesses diligently tried to keep up to our needs; we were boisterous, in good spirits but respectful of people around us.

Having played over forty games and after the tough rigorous schedules and matches during the previous nine months, we had trained hard, played hard and now we were intending to party hard, this was the carrot in front of the donkey's nose. The rules were simple; you had to go, it was compulsory, no excuses. Some were a little weak and tried to get out of the trip, these players were usually the ones who were pressurised from other sources not to join in, but the jibes from fellow players must have outweighed the opposition because until Super League came along it was rare for anyone to miss. The other rule was no cameras, what happens over in the Garden of Eden stayed in the Garden of Eden. I remember one young player who brought a camera on to the hotel patio and began snapping like a regular David Bailey. His face was the only real picture worth taking as he watched in shocked amazement, his jaw dropping as the camera, as if in slow motion, hurtled through the air then splashed into the pool, quickly sinking from view. We later learned that the auto exposure had been switched on during this mugging and the salvaged, later developed film, proved only to contain various shots of the newly tiled pool bottom.

One of my favourite recollections from these trips was from early on in my career. As a youngster, you had to be willing to be the butt of most jokes and japes from senior professionals and your acceptance into the upper hierarchy was judged on your ability to deal with the incidents. And many times, the beach, the sun and copious amounts of alcohol often brought about impromptu events - one such was when Gary Connell, a former Cas prop whose promising career was curtailed by injury, decided to challenge all comers to a sumo wrestling match. Of course, there were no takers, he had not earned the nickname 'The Fat Jap' for nothing. But as the amber nectars continued to flow I found enough Dutch courage to accept this continual barrage of challenges from Castleford's sumo champ elect, it would be the master versus the novice.

The rest of the lads quickly excavated a circular trench to form the arena, one player agreed to be my second and asked which corner I was in, I gave him a quizzical look and pointed out it was a circle. Meantime Gary was posturing across the ring like the legendary Dump Truck, hurling handfuls of sand across his mighty frame to compensate for the lack of salt, as with most beach events of this nature a crowd of fellow holidaymakers began to gather, curious that this ancient Japanese sport had emerged on a sun-kissed Magaluf beach. I have to admit Gary cut an imposing figure stepping in then out of the ring, into the crouching position, out of the crouching position, grunting and snarling followed by a wide-eyed stare across in my direction. My second, who still insisted he was in my corner, began covering my upper torso in sun tan lotion. The rest of the lads, plus the now sizeable audience were in hysterics, then silence ensued as I stepped into the ring, crouching and mimicking Gary stomping his feet. We now faced each other, our faces only two feet apart awaiting the sound of John Joyner's clap of his outstretched hands. CLAP - Gary lunged forward; I stepped to one side to then witness Gary's hands desperately trying to cling to my oil-covered torso. He staggered further forward then tumbled into the sand face first. The crowd roared their approval as I strutted, arms aloft. Gary jumped to his feet and pleaded, 'best of three, best of three', spluttering as he spat the sand from his mouth and complaining that I was covered in oil. John ordered me towelled down to remove the offending substance and once again, Gary began his pre-combat dance, this time his pride was at stake. Half crouched, we faced each other in front of a now ever increasing crowd loaded with enthusiastic onlookers, Gary began to milk the audience, raising his left knee almost above shoulder height and slamming it down into the hot sand, then with a mighty roar he raised his right knee to an even more exaggerated height. JJ's hands were ready to clap as Gary brought his right foot down only to scream out in agony, crumple into a heap then roll around clutching his lower leg, 'Oh my foot, my foot, it's fucking broke, it's broke.' People were rolling about laughing uncontrollably as Gary continued to curse and swear. At last, someone decided to investigate further, insisting to Gary to keep still whilst I scraped the sand away from the last impact area of his right foot. Sure enough, a thin covering of sand revealed a smooth massive rock, it was serious but not one of the lads could control their boisterous laughter. 'You bastards, help me across the prom to the bar.' Gary in his now authoritative voice boomed. We carried him and set him down in a chair, I elevated his leg, I then asked Mano the waiter to bring some ice for Gary's now massively swollen appendage. Gary then cried out, 'Mano, can you bring us fourteen bottles of San Miguel back with you when you bring the ice please? Thanks mate.' The hospital could obviously wait until the next day, Gary was carrying the kitty and his last words were, 'if you bastards leave me, I'll spend it all on myself.' There was laughter all round but nobody left the Fat Jap that night, broken foot or not.

Gradually the end of season trips have diminished, I tried to resurrect the days of old but ended up in Blackpool on my own (some would say with my mates), but the characters are fast diminishing from our game, mores the pity.

The following day, after demonstrating sumo wrestling on the Magalluf beach it was time to introduce rugby league. We had again spent a leisurely afternoon in our favourite sea front bar, soaking up the sun and a few lagers and as late afternoon approached together with a cooling breeze, the beach began to empty. I then spied a young Adonis using a rugby ball as a pillow and was despatched by the elders to approach the guy and borrow the ball for a game of touch and pass and after assuring him that we were professionals and we would not let the ball come to any harm, he reluctantly handed it over.

There was by now a vast expanse of open beach and the lads

proceeded to mark out a pitch of gym size proportions, two sides, five on each and it was game on, encouraged by the Fat Jap from the promenade bar plus a few who had declined to take part. A tidy gathering of promenade troopers had now halted and were watching us proceed with ever increasing expressions of incredulity. As the tempo of the game increased, both encouragement and abuse filled the air from our quickly converted fans, sweaty sun kissed bodies were rapidly changing colour from bronze to red as the taps became slaps, then the slaps became whacks, quickly followed by the inevitable booze induced full blown rugby. Big hits, diving try saving tackles, the crowd loved it, honest it was as intense as a Sky televised night at the Jungle. Shaun Irwin suffered a split lip, I a received a busted nose and I suspect the ale was clouding our judgement, then Johnny Wray received the ball, skipped his way past three defenders and dived over for the match clinching try. As we were deliriously celebrating, we failed to notice that Johnny was huddled in a heap. After concerned expressions of encouragement, we managed to haul him to his feet, bruised, totally dehydrated and gasping for air. Johnny was the fittest among us, so it was definitely game over but to our surprise and delight, we were applauded along the beach back to the bar by a hundred or so fellow holidaymakers. I returned the rugby ball to it's rightful owner and told him we would be having another game tomorrow if he wanted to join in. 'Er, no thanks, I play union, different rules you know.' I thanked him once again and made my way for some more amber nectar as the sun began to vanish beyond the horizon.

Some of my happiest memories have been from the end of season trips, all the pressures are off from playing and training and everyone can just relax, which is a great environment to be in, especially when there are real characters out there with you, the laughter seems to last all day. One year I was lucky to be with a real character, Tony 'Casper' Smith. Casper had never been out of the country before so it was like watching a kid in a sweet shop. We set up base in a hotel bar and pool complex at the end of the beach and at every opportunity Casper was continually pushing people in the pool, fully clothed or not. If you fell asleep beside the pool or just wanted to relax, then he'd be bombing into the water and soaking everyone wet through. This went on for a few days and one or two of the players were getting a little tired of it, myself included. A joke's a joke but this was getting ridiculous, so I decided to teach our Casper a lesson. One afternoon JJ asked Casper to go to the bar, he had to pass me on the way as I was positioned right beside the pool on a sun lounger, pretending to read the paper. Several minutes passed then I spied Casper returning, with a couple of bottles in each hand and his wallet in his mouth. As he drew level, I sprang forward and upwards, hitting my shoulder into his ribs, he had suspected nothing and as we hurtled into the pool, I took a deep breath, wrapped myself around Casper's body, and held him tight. WHOOSH! We hit the water and sank to the bottom of the pool, Casper was struggling wildly but was unable to shake my hold, I had a mouth full of air and Casper, with the surprise of what had happened, didn't. He turned, looked at me and the panic in his face told me that he'd learnt his lesson. I blew a few bubbles in his direction and he began to struggle again so I squeezed then released him. Casper scrambled to the surface gasping and coughing as he dragged himself from the water, I swam over to the side of the pool, climbed out and calmly sat back down on my sun lounger and for the first time that week relaxed. It was hilarious watching Casper trying to dry out his wallet.

One year I was rooming with Martin Ketteridge and Lee Crooks. Lee's wife Karen was expecting so he wasn't doing much boozing just in case he had to return home at short notice, but Ketts and I were certainly making up for him. We were about four days into the holiday, Ketts and I were having a light drinking session down at the beach bar, sitting opposite each other drinking cans of Bud then placing the empties on top of each other in the centre of the table. Our goal was to stop drinking and go home when we had consumed enough cans to obscure our view of each other. At seven o'clock, we had a leisurely stagger home, Crooksy wasn't in, probably phoning Karen to check everything was okay on the baby front. I had a nap then resurfaced around midnight, showered, changed, and made my way into town, still no sign of Lee. I met up with Ketts, we had a great night then headed home around seven o'clock in the morning. There was bright sunshine so that meant I could catch up on my sleep on the beach - couldn't miss out on the opportunity to top my tan up. As we climbed the hill back to our room a stream of water came cascading down the gutter in the road and as we grew closer we could hear the unmistakable sound of water falling on to concrete. 'Bit early to be watering the plants.' I commented. On reaching our apartments Ketts and I looked at each other then ran up the stairs to our room, sure enough the water was falling on the path below from our floor and the water from our floor was coming from our room. BANG, BANG, BANG. I crashed my fist onto the door. 'Crooksy, Crooksy, open the door.' I shouted. BANG, BANG, BANG. Then even louder. 'CROOKSY OPEN THIS BLOODY DOOR!' Silence then the sound of someone on the bed. 'What, who is it?' Crooksy replied. All we heard then was splashing and Crooksy going 'oh hell' over and over. The door swung open and a small tidal wave of water left the room, all our clothes, suitcases and furniture floating away right behind it, the water hit the floor below like machine gun fire, if there'd been an Aussie in the team he'd have ridden that wave all the way to Palma Nova. We salvaged our clothes and suitcases and I raised a few of the boys and the mopping up began. Thank God for tiled floors, no one was any the wiser to what had happened.

Turned out that Crooksy had become a father that night and everything being okay, he had gone out to wet the baby's head. Ketts, Lee and myself had been like ships in the night, so on Lee returning at about 1 am, he decided that he fancied a bath. The plug went in, on went the taps and the bath began to fill, Crooksy went back into the bedroom to get undressed, pants off, shirt off, one sock then ZZZZZ fast asleep on top of the bed, dead to the world. Six hours later and our own indoor swimming pool, again BANG, BANG, BANG.

29

Career Change

The hooter sounded at the JJB stadium, we were out of the Super League play-offs, then it hit me like a Mike Tyson right cross, it was over. My professional career as a player, sixteen years, seventeen seasons, 456 games, all ended at 7.42 pm on Saturday September 28th, 2002. I removed the headphones through which I had received Graham's instructions throughout the game and sat down. It was not the way I would have chosen to end my career as a non-playing member of the squad but I had received my accolades two weeks before, at least I had that memory, and it was time to let the boys enjoy it now. The story was at an end but at least after all these years I would again be able to don the red and black hoops of Stanley Rangers, the club I played for from ten years old.

My first game back was away at Moorends in Doncaster. I kept a low profile in the build up to the game but to be honest I was like a kid in a candy shop, then a 54-6 victory and a dream return - I even got over for a try. I hadn't enjoyed my rugby this much for a long time and I was bursting with enthusiasm. But many outside Stanley were waiting for me to fail, wondering if I'd gone soft and expecting me not to be able to cut-it now, however this just motivated me to try harder than ever because I hate losing at anything.

I guess when I returned to Stanley, I expected we would turn things around overnight, well that hasn't proved to be the case, but we are on the right track and with more hard work we will again be a successful side. No doubt with my reputation there were a few people waiting for me to be sent off, well, I had made a goal to myself to get to the end of the season without falling foul of the referees. I was under no illusion that I wouldn't come in for some special attention from opposing players and spectators wherever I played, but even I wasn't prepared for the amount of provocation that came my way and I think I did well to last six games before losing my rag.

I guess there are a number of players in the amateur ranks who think they can make a name for themselves by giving me some of the rough stuff, and no doubt as an ex-professional I am something of a target. Well that's okay, I'm a big boy and I can handle the special attention, but what I do object to is the moment I step outside the rules to retaliate or return some of the rough treatment, then I'm the one that gets the full force of the referees wrath. Maybe the Super League referees aren't so bad after all! Anyway, when I'm not playing with the Rangers, I occasionally turn out with my old mate Johnny Wray for Stanley Rodillians, my village rugby union club. It's an enjoyable game with a top bunch of blokes where I usually bag a try or two and come in for no extra attention from the opposition.

But then a final irony when in January 2003 Hull KR contacted me with an offer to play for them. I took the offer seriously, as dropping down a division would be easier on the body and because I believe Hull KR are a big enough club to mount a challenge for promotion. So I agreed to meet their new chief executive Nick Halafihi at a hotel near Brighouse to discuss the matter. Nick offered me terms, which included a big bonus if the club won the Grand Final and the package seemed fair to me so we shook hands on the deal.

Then the following day Nick phoned and said, 'Dean, there's a slight hiccup, the board have asked that I just make a few alterations'.

'Such as?'

'Nothing too drastic, it mainly relates to the incentive bonus, I have to get you to accept them cutting it.'

'Well that's unusual; boards of directors normally enjoy paying out incentive bonuses.'

'If I keep the deal within these revised terms will you still sign tomorrow?'

'Yes I have broken the news to my family and Dad has gone for a pint so he will have told half the village by now.'

I caught up with Dad in the village local and told him about the phone call, he was calm and collected and quickly reassessed what it meant in monetary terms, then he came out with one of his profound beauties. 'A hand shake or a written contract, they are worth sod all in rugby league, but you've still agreed to sign?'

'Yes the agreement stands.' I replied.

'Have you told anyone at Cas?'

'Only Tony Marchant my co-coach.'

Our conversation was interrupted by my mobile phone ringing. I answered and it was Nick again, his voice was hardly audible and his strained emotion alarmed me. 'They have withdrawn the offer Dean, completely taken it off the table.'

I knew Nick was gutted and so was I; throughout all of my dealings with Nick Halafihi I have found him to be of the highest integrity and I had not changed my opinion regardless of this devastating news. I stepped back to the bar and answered Dad's inquisitive look. 'They have withdrawn the offer in total it's no longer on the table.'

'Dad smiled. 'We've had worse knocks son, little do they know it's their loss.'

That night we had a good drink, me, Dad and Uncle Malcolm. I was quite philosophical; hopefully I had not burned my bridges with Cas but what if I had resigned my position? Would Hull KR have hung me out to dry? It is disconcerting that simply by loving the game so much and wanting to continue playing I had exposed my wife and family to the prospect of immeasurable hardships. I ask myself had the worst scenario evolved, would the handshake have stood up in court. For that was potentially a course of action facing me and if successful would I have been blacklisted, prevented from ever fulfilling my dream of becoming a successful first class coach? I don't know why the deal fell through but I suspect it was my request for a personal guarantee from the board that my contract would be honoured if I honoured my side, alas we will never know. I believe a newspaper in Hull indicated I had priced myself out of a deal, not so, I had accepted what I was offered, but no problem, I'm sure life has other adventures in store.

Anyway I'm now enjoying my new role as a player performance manager whilst coaching the youngsters at Cas. I hope that I can progress through the coaching ranks and maybe one day I can emulate the great Mal Reilly and lead Castleford out into the new Wembley stadium. I believe I have the ability to get to the top again, I know I have the will to succeed, I just hope one day, with an ounce of luck, that I am given the opportunity.

Postscript

Sometimes when I'm in a reflective mood, I feel I can almost taste my ancestral past, it's surreal, it's like I can transpose myself back in time, I turn off the TV and sit in a candlelit room everyone's in bed and yet everyone's here. Huddled around a roaring coal fire listening to my ancestors conversations, they can't see me but I'm with them, uncomplicated people who asked for and had very little. Even in those days when life was often cheap my ancestors would still value it, I just know they would.

It's no doubt influenced by my dad relaying to me the stories of our family past, just his dad did to him. My great great great granddad, William, worked down the mines from being a young boy, probably alongside his father, only to die before his time. I often try to imagine the lives of the people of those times, mundane days from morning until night, long and arduous, hewing and carting coal for a pittance and after such back breaking fourteen hour shifts, returning home to the collective sound of clogs on cobbles, making concerto like arrangements to the ears of avaricious mine owners. Then a pitiful broth and after that, a brief interlude as a family before off to bed in cold, damp rooms, several to a bed dreaming of Sunday and a day of rest.

These humbling thoughts are the things I have drawn on during such needy occasions, and afterwards I feel I have been through a cleansing process, it is certainly good therapy when feeling low. Sometimes it leaves me feeling a little guilty that I have been able to play a game that I love for so long and be well paid for it. Then I remind myself and take consolation that if there is a God and they're all in heaven looking over the balcony cheering me on, then I hope they realise that it was through their toil and sacrifice that I'm where I am today.

Both Dad and I agree that for many different reasons, publishing our personal stories was the right thing to do and we believe it was also done in the right way by being honest and forthright in our opinions. We hope we have given readers a true insight into our lives and that they have been able to identify in some ways with us. We are just working class people, who have a natural trait to try to succeed in whatever we attempt, be it sport, business or whatever. Making decisions on which path to take and then if it has been the wrong one, then we have paid the price without complaint. And if we feel an injustice has been committed, we have fought back and if we have lost then we have tried to retain our dignity.

New offspring are constantly being brought into the world by brothers, sisters and cousins and because of our books and Dads effort to finally log our family tree, those future generations will be able to share in our family past and that alone is reward enough. If people stop me in the street as I have seen so many do to Dad and state that they have read my biography, then that will be an added bonus and if they say they have enjoyed the story of our lives and fortunes then so much the better.

To quote my dad, and I know he's quoting Granddad, 'it's all character building, that's how the Sampson family are'. Whenever anything drastic occurs in the family, be it a physical injury or a personal dilemma, that old adage comes out once again. Well my experiences since March 13th, 2001 should have me bursting with bloody character. First the shock of the bankruptcy and coping with the consequences, then a double hernia operation and its complications and finally negotiating a new contract with Cas. I certainly had to dig deep into my reserves, especially to generate the enthusiasm needed to reach the fitness levels required for Super League VII. But what goes around comes around and Dad and I were recently informed by our new solicitors that we have a case for suing the solicitor who handled our bankruptcy and that we stand a good chance for annulment and compensation. It won't be resolved overnight but we are quietly optimistic.

This last year has certainly been eventful, my Aunt Maire in Canada had yet another heart attack, also my Uncle Brian collapsed after rushing to watch my cousin Paul play for Wasps against London Irish and then had to endure a triple heart bypass. What's really ironic is he had only just been informed that he was all clear after his three year battle with cancer. Talk about out of the frying pan and into the fire, and I think I've had it tough. Well I suppose I have, but I must feed from what is ahead of me and the example set by others, especially my mum and my sister Rebecca, who have quietly gone through all the recent traumas without a single whinge. Both have had to put their lives on hold, and would have had every justification for griping long, loud and often. But neither have, and both have given Dad their full support, gradually helping him to reassert himself. I just hope the dogged determination he has shown will in time reap its rewards.

I believe everyone has a purpose, it may well be different for each of us but I feel that we should try to live our lives with at least one common aim, to try to ensure our offspring and others too are entering a world that will be better for our efforts. I know that in some small ways my own family before and during my lifetime have made many small contributions to our village of Lee Moor, Stanley. Although our village has expanded beyond recognition, Lee Moor is still fringed by green open spaces. Its high plateau can be walked daily and the fresh air is there for all to enjoy. What it looked like two or three hundred years ago must have been breathtaking, before first the mines and now industrial estates began blotching and scarring the landscapes. My great great granddad married his wife Sarah Smales in Lee Moor in 1858, he at this time had been down those mines for six years as had his dad William before him. They had toiled long hours underground for a pittance, but how they must have enjoyed Sundays, large families, summer sunshine and fresh air into wheezing lungs. William died in 1850 aged only forty-seven, having worked down the mine along with his father and brothers too. So in their small way, along with a few other long standing Lee Moor'ites, they began to form a community that has blossomed a little more each decade. The Lindleys, Firths, Broadheads, Wards, Woods and Lands are but a few of the many family names to evolve and then spread like the great oak. My great great uncles, William and Charles moved to the Smawthorne area of Castleford before the turn of the twentieth century, I hope one day to find their ancestral tree and check for living relatives. We recently found their burial site, unmarked of course, indicative of poverty of those times but it seems ironic that both Dad and myself trained many times near that same cemetery without ever realising that two uncles and an aunt were at rest close by.

Dad informs me that he's completed our family tree, not just our direct lineage, he has done the lot; uncles, aunts and their ancestors. He rang a Trevor Sampson in Methley and found out that Charles who Dad had traced to the cemetery was his granddad. He gave the whole picture and he commented how pleased he was to be related to us having often wondered. Dad's long held theory that the many local Sampson families were connected was proven correct, Roy Sampson who coaches at Hunslet and his brother Ian who played with Dad are now proven distant relatives, so too Trevor Sampson who played with uncle Malcolm at Wakefield Trinity. So the sporting prowess in Dad's book has a new found expansive nature to it. Let's just hope our children can continue to aspire to sporting fame because it's surely in the genes.

Dad has said that a certain Clement Sampson, another distant relative, was president of not only the Federation of Yorkshire Supporters Clubs but also he was president of the Castleford Supporters Club and a doorman and projectionist at a couple of local Cas cinema's. It turns out he shared his doorman duty with the immortal Arthur Atkinson which puts icing on the cake for me. His son Ray has recently been in contact with Dad, he too a lifelong Cas supporter, we were all unaware of our close links with Castleford past and present until now. It's a pity it wasn't done years ago so my granddad could have proudly enriched his life amongst his Castleford cousins, still better late than never.

Well I'm now starting my new career and Dad has recently made another debut - at a Bramley reunion dinner as an after dinner speaker. Fortunately, he lasted longer than the three minutes on his debut for Wakefield Trinity at Hunslet Parkside. He reckoned he was nervous before the event but the family all believe he was just seeking attention because we can't usually stop him talking about the old days in rugby or spouting opinions about the game today.

Well that's about everything from both Dad's story and mine. From telling my tale I am now more aware of the ideals regarding a visit to Shangri-La, Dad states visits to this mysterious place are enriching but not always enjoyable but if you're able to appraise and be self analytical about events in your life then so much the better. On our journey, we have covered over forty years of life in rugby league and we have tried to share not only the sport but also the story of our family life through the generations - just like any other normal working class family and I can only hope you too have enjoyed the ride alongside us.

Tributes

Stuart Raper

It was a very interesting and indeed, exciting time when I joined Castleford as coach in 1997, the club was staring relegation in the face and I knew that I had to call on the experience of all the older pro's of which Diesel was one. His contribution went a long way to securing Castleford's place in Super League. In my time at Cas, Diesel was one rare breed - a prop that could last eighty minutes and you could always guarantee that whilst he was out there he would give 100%. Diesel and I had the occasional, professional differences but there was a special relationship of respect and no matter what happened between us, he would always be one of the first names on my team sheet. The relationship between Diesel and I was probably helped by some of the afternoons spent in the judiciary at Red Hall! He was certainly a fiery character on the pitch and we had to spend plenty of time together as a result of his wholehearted approach to the sport and the club he loves. Diesel probably didn't get the accolades or representative honours he deserved but as a coach you know that when he pulls on the shirt he will give everything to the cause.

One of the hardest ever defeats during my time at Castleford was the 1999 Challenge Cup semi-final against London Broncos and I will never forget the look on Dean's face and how the loss affected him. Typical Diesel though, he hit back the week after and this incident really sticks in my mind. We had a tough game with Halifax which was made all the more important after the cup setback, the season could have gone either way but right at the end of a real seesaw battle, Diesel produced a shoulder charge that dislodged the ball from a Halifax player's grasp which enabled Adrian Vowles to score the winning try. From that point, we went on to make the play-offs and came within a whisker of the Grand Final.

Although a prop forward, his strength enabled him to find the try line more than any other prop I have ever seen and I'll never forget his first half hat-trick in a 32-32 draw with St Helens at Knowsley Road.

I would like to wish Diesel all the best with whatever he does in the future, he has had plenty of ups and downs in his career and that often produces a character which Diesel certainly is, he is also a character I can call a friend.

John Kear

I am very honoured to have been asked to contribute to Dean's autobiography; I have known Dean since the mid eighties when I finished playing and started my coaching career. Deano always has had a massive influence on any team, even as a youngster in a very good reserve side he made a big impact and as reserve team coach I was always pushing for his inclusion into the first team, however he had one big barrier to overcome, his dad, Dave, who was then the first team coach. As Dave constantly told me, 'for a father to pick his son in a professional sport he not only has to be playing well but has to be playing twice as well as his competitors'. Well thankfully for all at Cas over the past years, Deano did that and played so well his dad had no option but to play him and the rest is history, an all time great in the Cas playing ranks.

Everybody who has Cas at heart will have to pay tribute to a great prop and I feel privileged to know Dean and to having been associated with such a top bloke who has always given his best for Castleford out on the playing field. Well-done Deano and good look for the future, which I'm sure will be as colourful and successful as the past has been.

Mick Morgan

In November 1965, I put pen to paper, signing the dotted line for Wakefield Trinity and this was my first introduction to the Sampson family; Brian, Malcolm and David. Brian was the eldest brother; chief steward, extra's organiser for the filming of This Sporting Life and self-proclaimed guru of his two younger brothers, both established first teamer's at Trinity, Malc at prop and Dave at centre. Now here is the first twist in the tail, I too played centre and our contemporaries who we were vying with were the likes of Neil Fox, Ian Brooke and Tony Thomas. Ironic really that David and myself were to finish our careers playing prop where Malc had started so many years before.

It was February 1986, some twenty years later that David and myself again became allies, I signed for Cas to run the commercial department and double up helping with on field development of the A-team who were coached by none other than Dave. Also at the club was Dean Sampson, a fresh-faced young teenager at prop. Then one season on, Mal Reilly took the Great Britain coaching job and David stepped up to take his place. In the interim, Dean had come on in leaps and bounds, once scoring three tries against Wakefield at Belle Vue. I vividly remember stressing to Dave that he should give the lad a chance and this was endorsed by John Kear. But I believe Dave didn't want accusing of nepotism so early in the season although he relented when I suggested he might be holding him back. When Dave handed Dean his debut he had a big match and scored the game breaking try, he had arrived big style.

Pre-Super League the game was part-time and players often supplemented their incomes with casual or full-time employment, and like everyone else, Dean would inevitably make mistakes at work or in his game but he learned the hard way of never tell your team mates of errors committed. One day he explained he had been given a simple driving task with the family business; 'pick up these materials and put some juice in the tank,' simple orders lacking one vital instruction, petrol or diesel. Well Dean got it wrong, he opted for diesel and innocently confided in his fellow gladiators, silly lad, hence the name Diesel, as he has been known ever since.

I've had the privilege of seeing Diesel blossom throughout his long loyal career which has seen him gain representative honours and enjoy being a part of the elevated times such as the Regal Trophy, Wembley, Yorkshire Cup and Premierships. But that's only half the story for this affable prop who has now completed sixteen seasons as a one club man, has demonstrated his loyalty, durability and integrity like no other in the game today.

Richard Wright

As Chief Executive of Castleford Tigers the tasks I become involved in are wide ranging but I would have to say that my dealings with Diesel have certainly been some of the more interesting parts of the job. We had many battles over team winning bonuses in his role as player's representative and I would have to say that never was the player's argument put more eloquently or forcefully, usually resulting in us paying more than we wanted. He did a superb job and I know he was a bit miffed when the players sacked him from the job in the 2002 season, they thought he had one foot in opposition's camp having taken on a coaching role as well as playing but in my opinion their worries were unfounded. One day Dean came into the office with a large photo of himself stood over Willie Poaching who was laid out cold during a game with Wakefield here at The Jungle. Willie had felled Brad Davis with a late shot after Brad had kicked the ball down field and Dean had retaliated; a young Tigers fan had sent him the photo and asked him to sign it. I was very dubious at first about him signing it but then Dean produced a letter he had written to the youngster explaining how sorry he was for his actions, which were a poor example of on the field behaviour. This incident typifies the person Dean is; always ready to stand up for the little guy, always ready to accept punishment when he occasionally breaks the rules, but always someone you want in your team. Dean has been a tremendous player, servant and ambassador for Castleford and has many admirable qualities, the fans love him and opponent's fans, players and officials have great respect for him, I am proud to know him and wish him every success in the future.

Adrian Vowles

I first met Diesel in 1990 at the Gold Coast Seagulls where he had an off-season stint for a few months. He had long hair (I think mullets were all the rage back then) and he was a lot smaller than he is now. For the first few months, no one actually understood a word he said because of his broad Yorkshire accent but he was quite liked by the club. I was only nineteen at the time and in my first year with The Seagulls so I thought it was great that I was able to train and play footy with a real life pommy and it wasn't long before I learnt my first bit of Yorkshire twang; 'hey up'. We played a few games together that year and it was a learning curve for both of us, especially when we were both in hot water for ordering a seafood platter the night before a game at about $40 per head and charging it to the club.

Our paths crossed again a few years later when Dean went to Parramatta and to be quite honest I thought that would be the last time I would see him. I don't think Dean or myself would have imagined when we met in 1990 that we would be team mates at Castleford seven years later but that is exactly what happened when I signed for the 1997 season. I must say it was great to see a familiar face when I first arrived and although we had a very tough season, we both earned the respect of each other and that has continued to this day. In the five years I had at Cas, Diesel very rarely failed to lead from the front and I am sincere when I say this that he should have been the first front rower picked for either Great Britain or England but somehow his face did not fit the picture. But I think Dean can still look back at his career now he has finally retired and be very proud of what he has achieved because for a front rower to play as many games as he has at Cas is an honour in itself and I doubt it will be beaten. My only regret and I know it is Diesel's too, is we didn't make it to Wembley in 1999 when we were beaten by London in the last few minutes at Headingley, there were a few tears shed by me and Dean that day but it just wasn't meant to be.

On a lighter note, Dean hurt his leg one day at The Jungle when we were playing St Helens and had to be stretchered off. The crowd were chanting his name over and over, he was obviously very happy with this because he made the blokes who were carrying him take him around the field four times before disappearing into the tunnel.

Dean I would like to firstly thank you for asking me to write this for you and secondly to say it has been an honour to play side-by-side with you and I hope your coaching career one day opens a door for you to be head coach at Castleford.

Appendix

Dean Sampson Career Statistics

Signed Professional	June 1986
1st Team Debut	August 1987
Appearances	427
Tries	68

Season	Played	Subbed	Tries	Points
1987/88	10	13	2	8
1988/89	14	13	7	28
1989/90	29	5	8	32
1990/91	34	1	2	8
1991/92	19	11	1	4
1992/93	21	13	2	8
1993/94	19	12	6	24
1994/95	30	-	11	44
1995/96	13	3	1	4

Season	Played	Subbed	Tries	Points
1996/97	9	9	2	8
1997	21	1	1	4
1998	22	-	6	24
1999	36	-	5	20
2000	21	3	7	28
2001	23	2	6	24
2002	8	12	1	4
Total	329	98	68	272

Other Appearances

	Year	Matches played
Gold Coast Seagulls	1990	12
Parramatta Eels	1995	8
Great Britain Tests	1997	1
Breat Britain Lions	1992	2
England	1995 & 1999	5
Great Britain U21's	1988	1
Total Appearances	1986/2002	456

Honours

Regal Trophy Winner	1993/94
Yorkshire Cup Winner	1990/91, 1991/92
Challenge Cup Runner-up	1991/92
Yorkshire Cup Runner-up	1987/88, 1988/89
Premiership Runner-up	1993/94
World Cup Runner-up	1995

Credits

Alliance Player of the Year	1986, 1987
1st Team Player of the Year	1990, 1997
1st Team Players Player	1990, 1997, 1999
1st Team Coach's Player	1990, 1997, 1999
1st Team Forward of the Year	1998
Past Players Association Player of the Year	1997
Super League Dream Team No10	1999

OTHER PUBLICATIONS

Fast Lane to Shangri-La
The Story of a Rugby League Family
Author: Dave Sampson
ISBN: 1-904091-00-8
Price: £9.99. Softback
Dave Sampson's autobiography captures the essence of rugby league and mixes it with a good dose of northern humour.

Just Champion!
Yorkshire's 33-Year Fight for their Cricketing Birthright
Author: David Bond
ISBN: 1-904091-03-2
Price: 14.99. Hardback
David Bond tells the story of the internal power struggle and internecine warfare as Yorkshire County Cricket Club battled to regain the County Championship.

Salford City Reds
A Willows Century
Author: Graham Morris
ISBN: 1-904091-02-4
Price: £18.99. Hardback, large format
The definitive illustrated history of Salford City Reds and their famous stadium.

Who Let the Dogs Out
The Revival of Newport Rugby
Author: Steve Lewis
ISBN: 1-904091-01-6
Price: £15.99. Hardback
Steve Lewis tells the story of how Newport Rugby fought back from the brink of obscurity to win the Principality Cup in 2001 and just miss out on the league title in 2002.

Coming soon

Kevin Ward; The Beast
Authors: Kevin Ward and Dave Sampson
ISBN: 1-904091-08-3
Price: £10.99. Softback
The autobiography of one of the all time greats of rugby league. A Castleford, St Helens and Manly legend.
Due out autumn/winter 2003

Taming the Tourists
How Cardiff Beat the All Blacks, Springboks and Wallabies
Author: Alan Evans
ISBN: 1-904091-06-7
Price: £15.99. Hardback
The epic tale of how one club beat the might of New Zealand, South Africa and Australia for a century and how the Wallabies lost to the Blue and Blacks six times in a row.
Due out autumn/winter 2003

Hull City
The Wilderness Years
Author: David Bond
ISBN: 1-904091-07-5
Price: £15.99. Hardback
The story of the most turbulent period in Hull City's existence and how this sleeping giant of football is at last starting to fight back from the brink.
Due out autumn/winter 2003

Vertical Editions titles can be purchased or ordered from your local bookshop, alternatively you can order direct. Send a cheque payable to Vertical Editions for the price of the book together with your name and delivery address to:

VERTICAL EDITIONS,
18-20 BLACKWOOD HALL LANE,
LUDDENDENFOOT, HALIFAX HX2 6HD
Free delivery in the UK